Alexander
BORODIN

SYMPHONY
No. 1
(1867)

Study Score
Partitur

SERENISSIMA MUSIC, INC.

ORCHESTRA

2 Flutes, 2 Oboes (2nd doubles as English Horn), 2 Clarinets, 2 Bassoons
4 Horns, 2 Trumpets, 3 Trombones
Timpani
Violin I, Violin II, Viola, Violoncello, Double Bass

Duration: ca. 31 minutes

Premiere: December 23, 1868
St. Petersburg, Russian Musical Society
Orchestra / Mily Balakirev

ISBN: 1-932419-72-1
This score is a slightly modified unabridged reprint of the score
published ca.1946 by Muzgiz (USSR State Publishing House)
The score has been reduced to fit the present format.

Printed in the USA
First Printing: January, 2009

SYMPHONY No. 1

Alexander Borodin
Edited by N. Rimsky-Korsakov and A. Glazunov

I

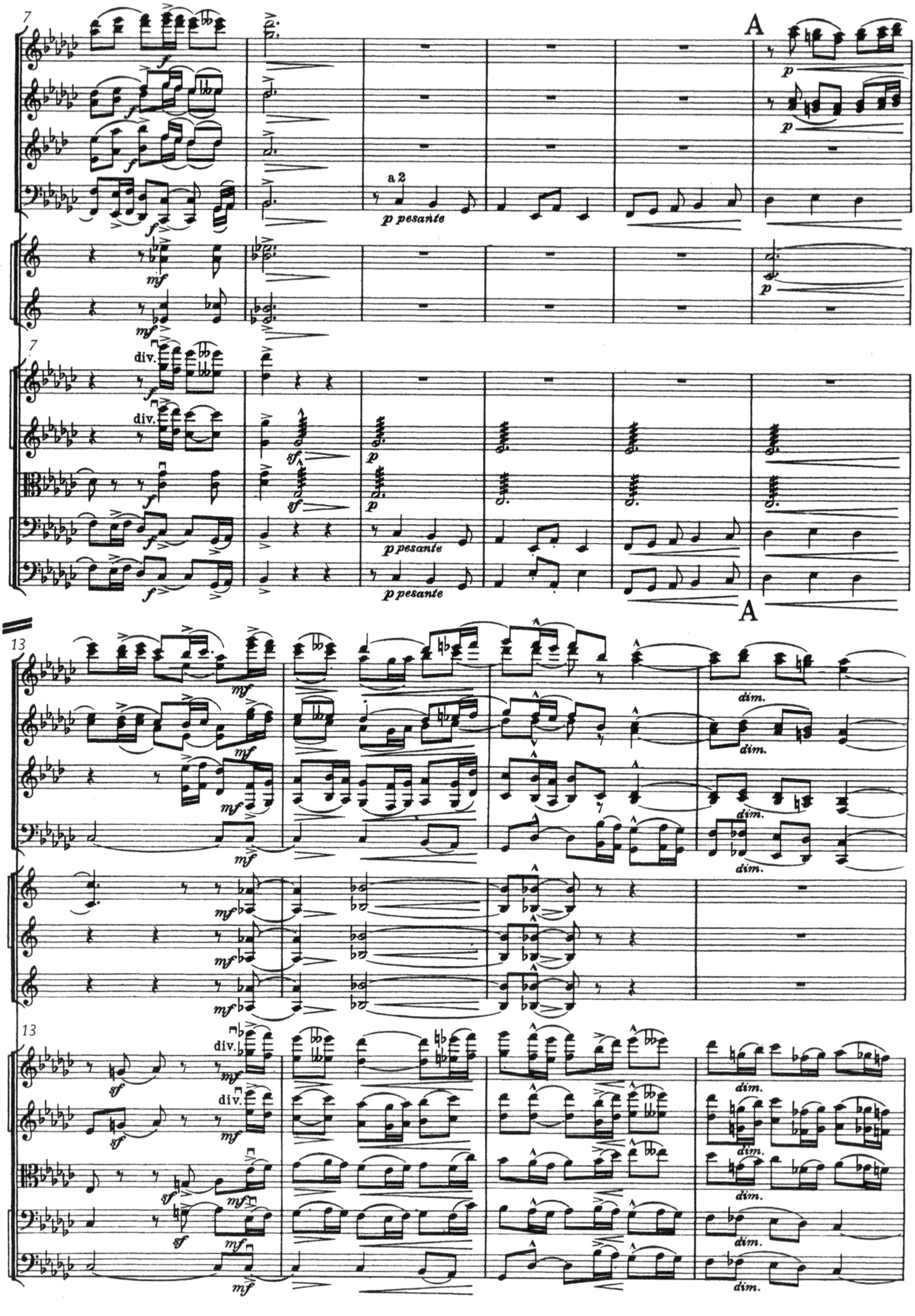
7
A
a 2
p pesante
div.
f
mf
p
sf
13
dim.

17
I.II Cor. in Es
a2
p marc.
pizz.
arco
p cresc.
23
a2
cresc.
mf cresc.
dim.
Cor. in Es
Timp.
pp cresc.

Allegro M.M. 𝅗𝅥 = 184
29
Cor. in Es
29
Allegro M.M. 𝅗𝅥 = 184
35
cresc.
cresc.
cresc. poco a poco
35

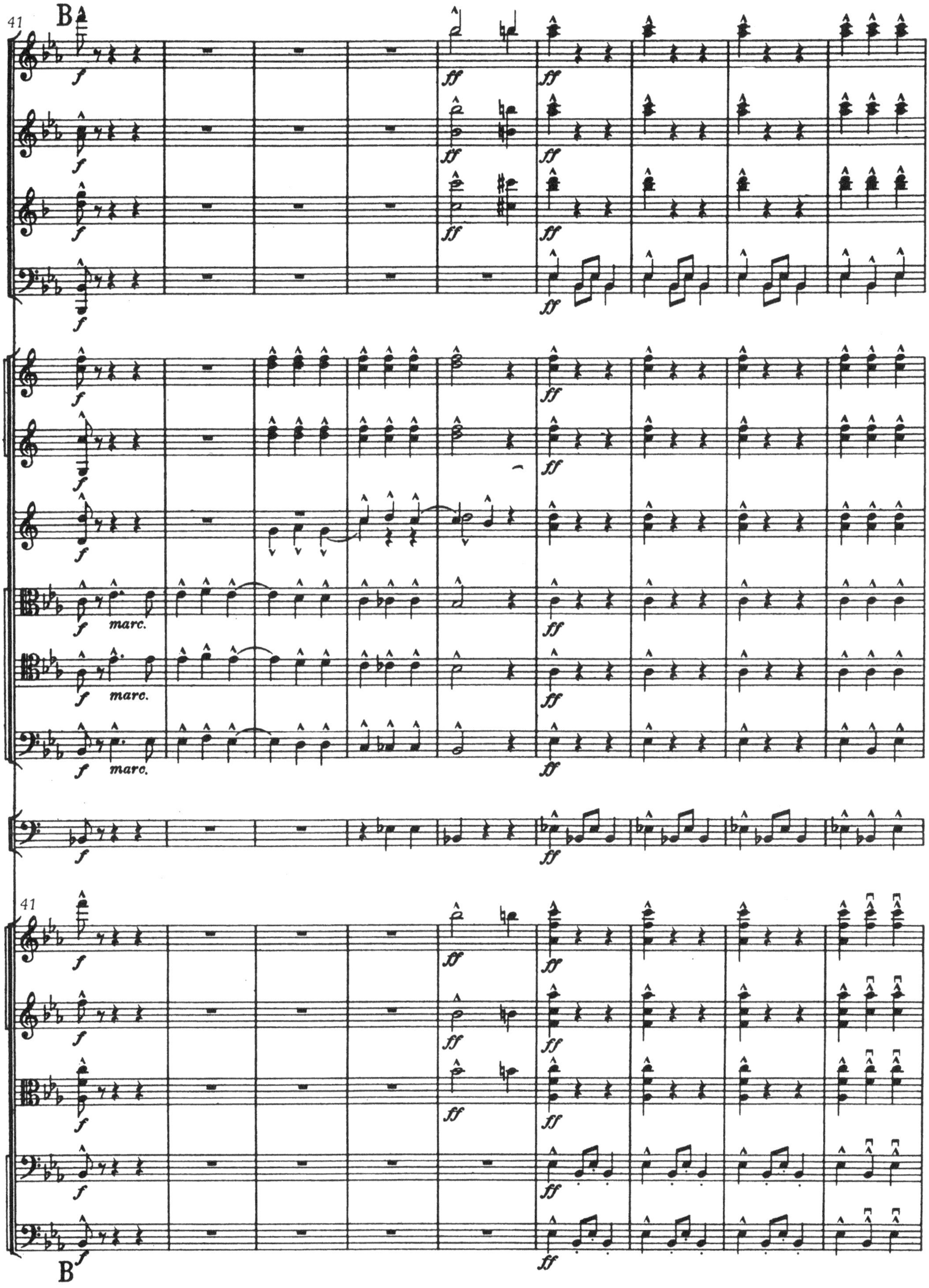
41
B
f
ff
marc.
41
B

8

56
C
Vl. I
Vl. II
Vle.
Vc.
Cb.
C
62
Ob.
I Solo
Fag.
Cor. in Es
Trbe in Es
Timp.
62
p legg. spiccato assai
p legg. spiccato assai
p legg. spiccato assai

68
Clar. in B
p
p
pp
68
pizz.
pp
pp
cresc. poco a poco
cresc. poco a poco
arco
p
cresc. poco a poco
p
cresc. poco a poco
74
Fl.
I
mf
f
p
f
f
f
p
Fag.
mf
f
I Solo
p
f
f
Trbe in Es
f
f
74
p
mf
f
f
f
pizz.
f
pizz.
f

80
p
I Solo
p
cresc. poco a poco
cresc. poco a poco
I
p
cresc. poco a poco
II Solo
p
pp cresc.
80
p
p
arco
mf
p
mf
86
a 2
mf
f
a 2
mf
a2
f
f
Trbe in Es
f
p
f
86
div.
mf
f
div.
mf
f
div.
mf
f
mf
f
arco
mf
f

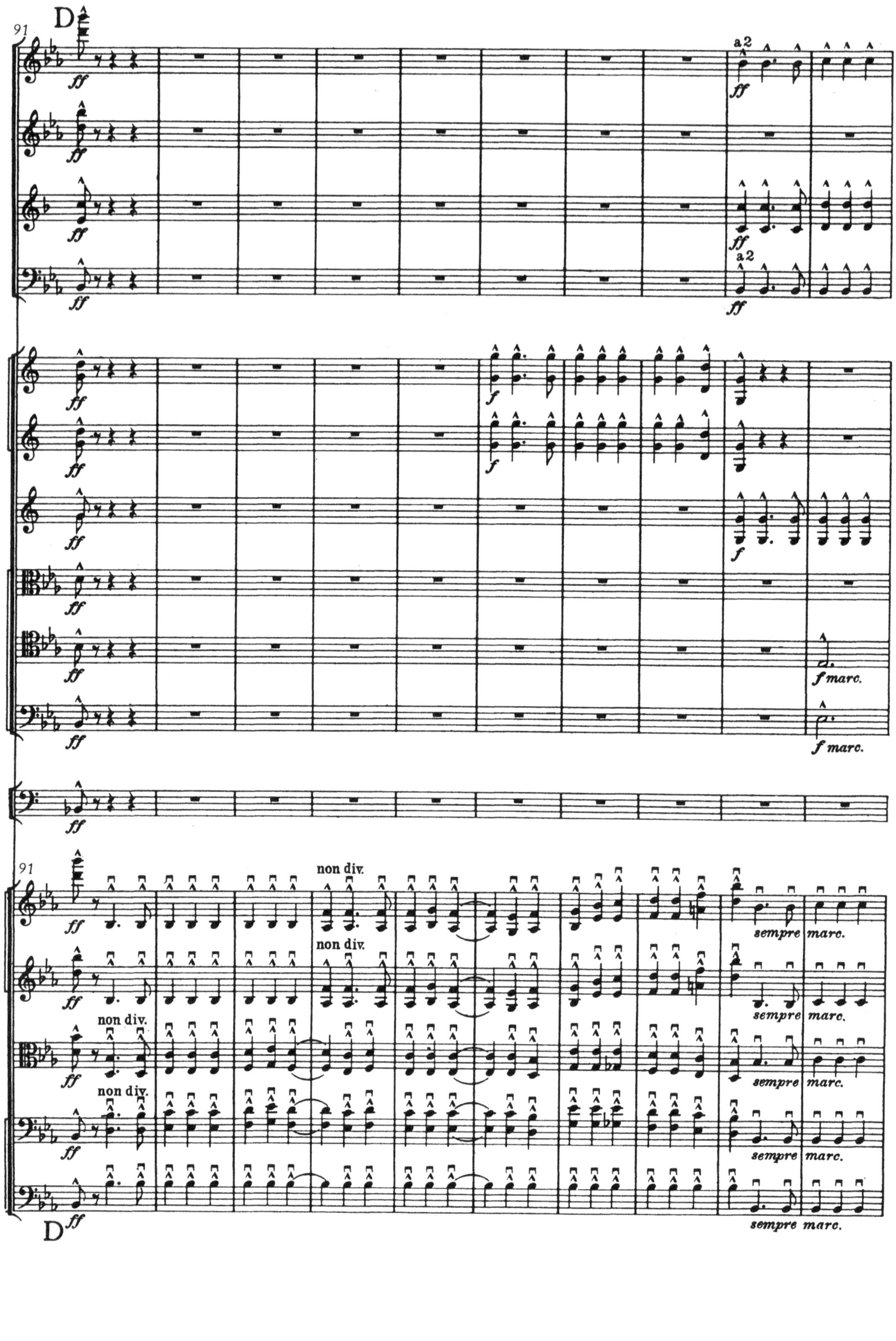
D
91
ff
a 2
f
f marc.
non div.
sempre marc.
D

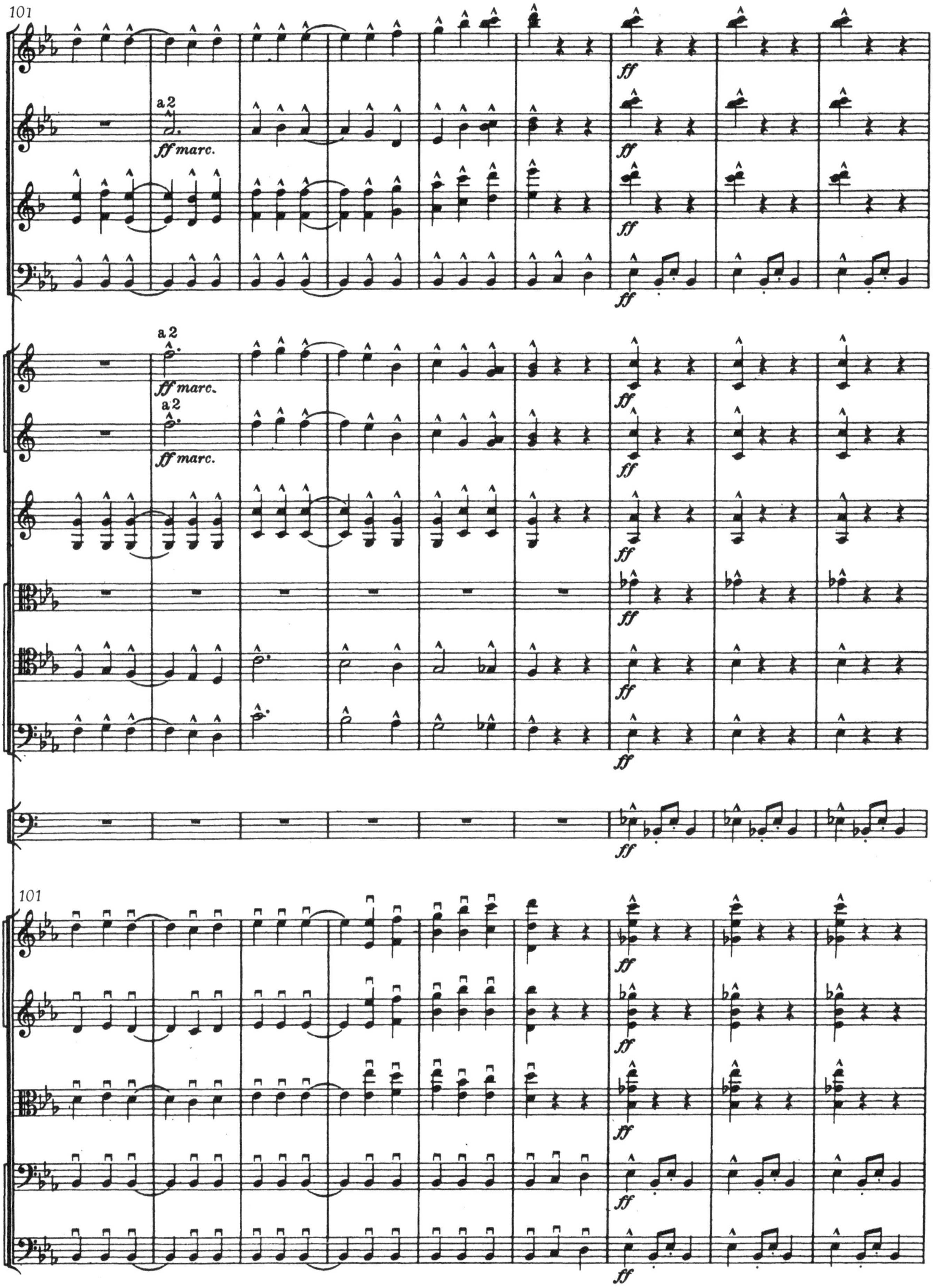
101
a 2
ff marc.
ff
a 2
ff marc.
a 2
ff marc.
101

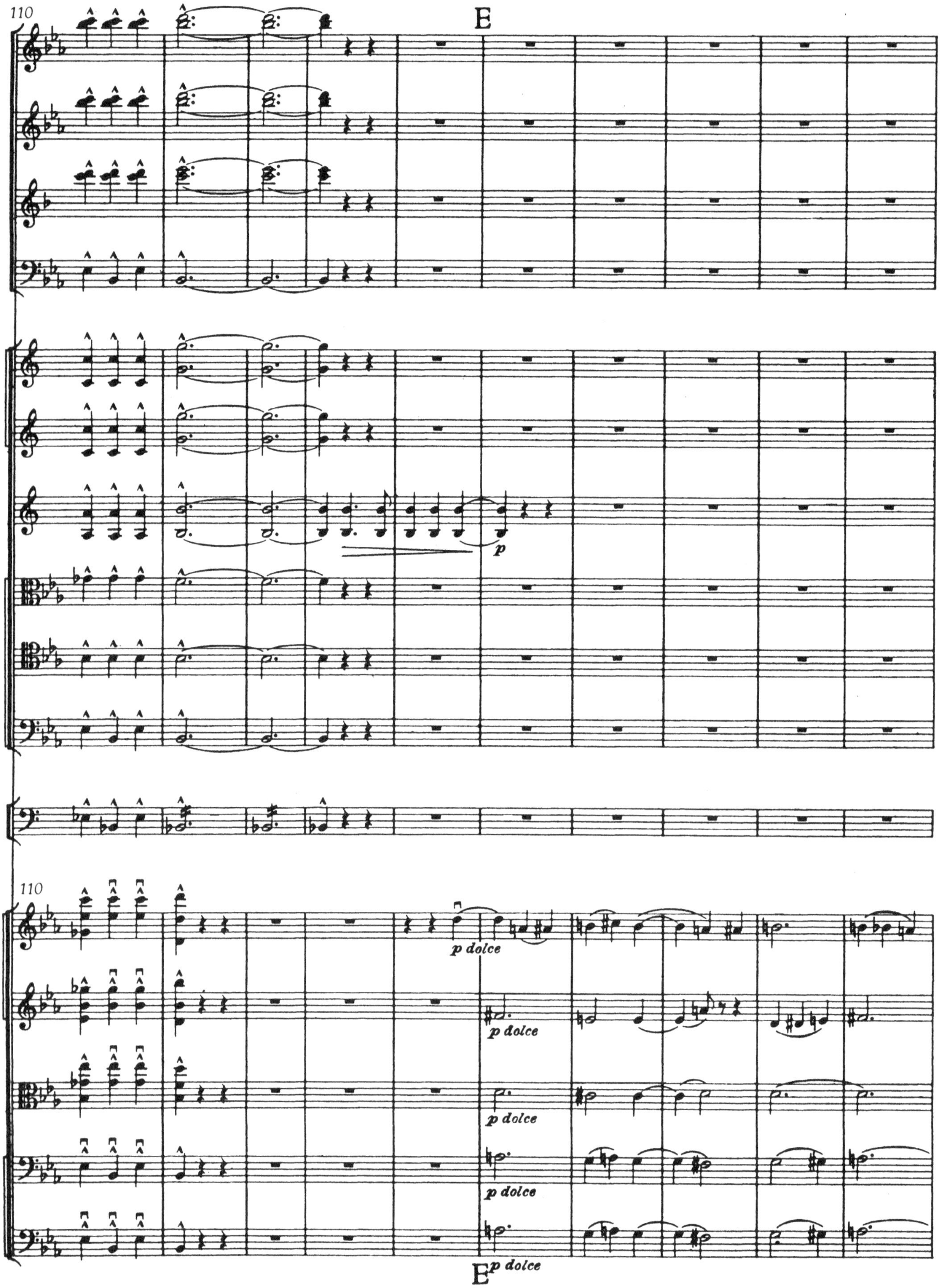
110
E
p
110
p dolce
p dolce
p dolce
p dolce
E p dolce

120
Fl.
Clar. in B
Cor. in Es
p
pp
sf
131
F
Ob. I
Fag.
p dolce
a 2
mf marc.
div. arco
pizz.

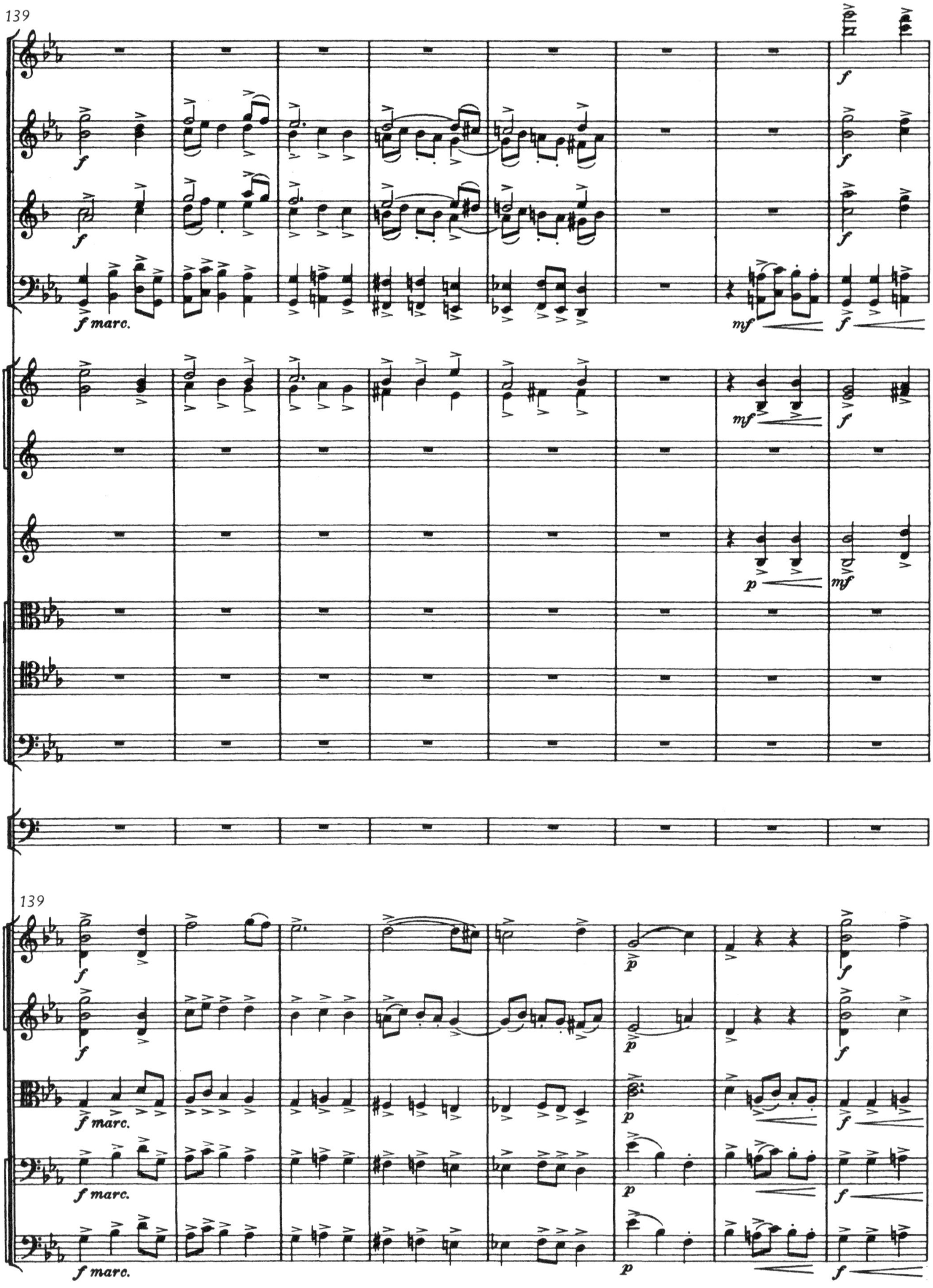
139
f marc.
139
f marc.
f marc.
f marc.

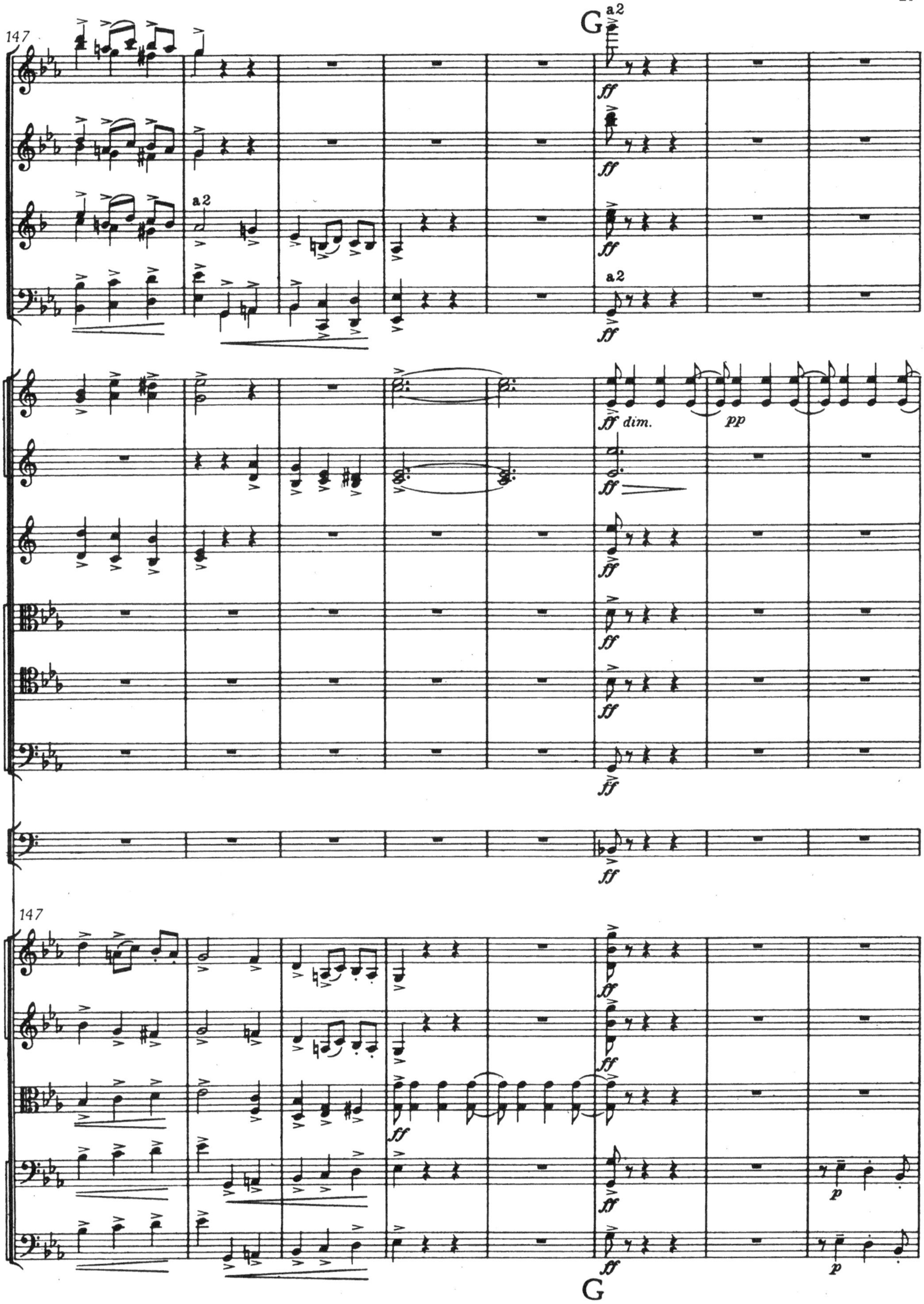
147
G
a2
ff
a2
dim.
pp
147
ff
p
G

155
Fag.
mf
p cresc. poco a poco
cresc. poco a poco
155
p
cresc. poco a poco
p
cresc. poco a poco
mf
cresc. poco a poco
cresc. poco a poco
162
f marc.
f marc.
f marc.
f
f
f
162
f
f
cresc.
f

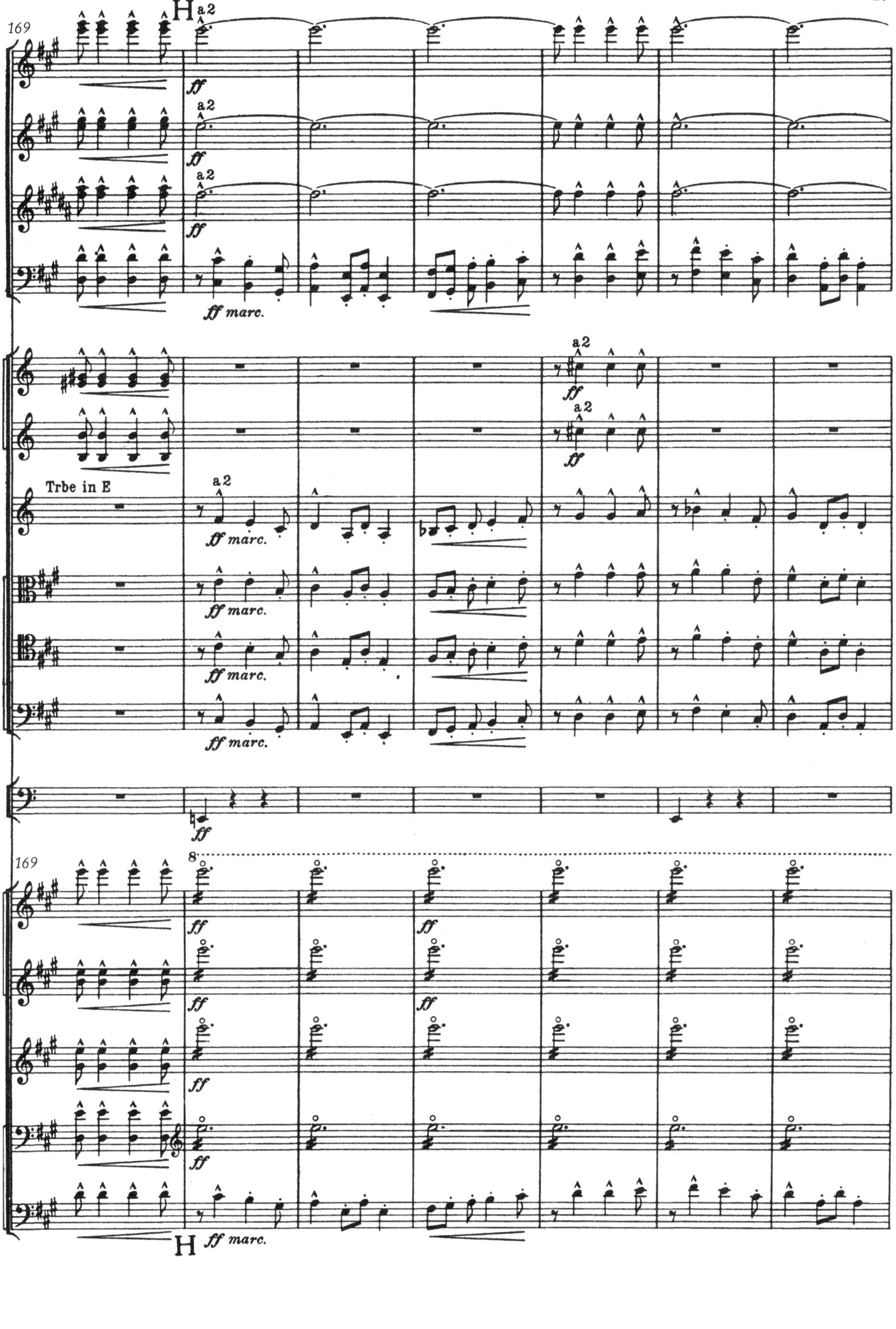
169
H
a 2
ff
ff marc.
Trbe in E
8
H

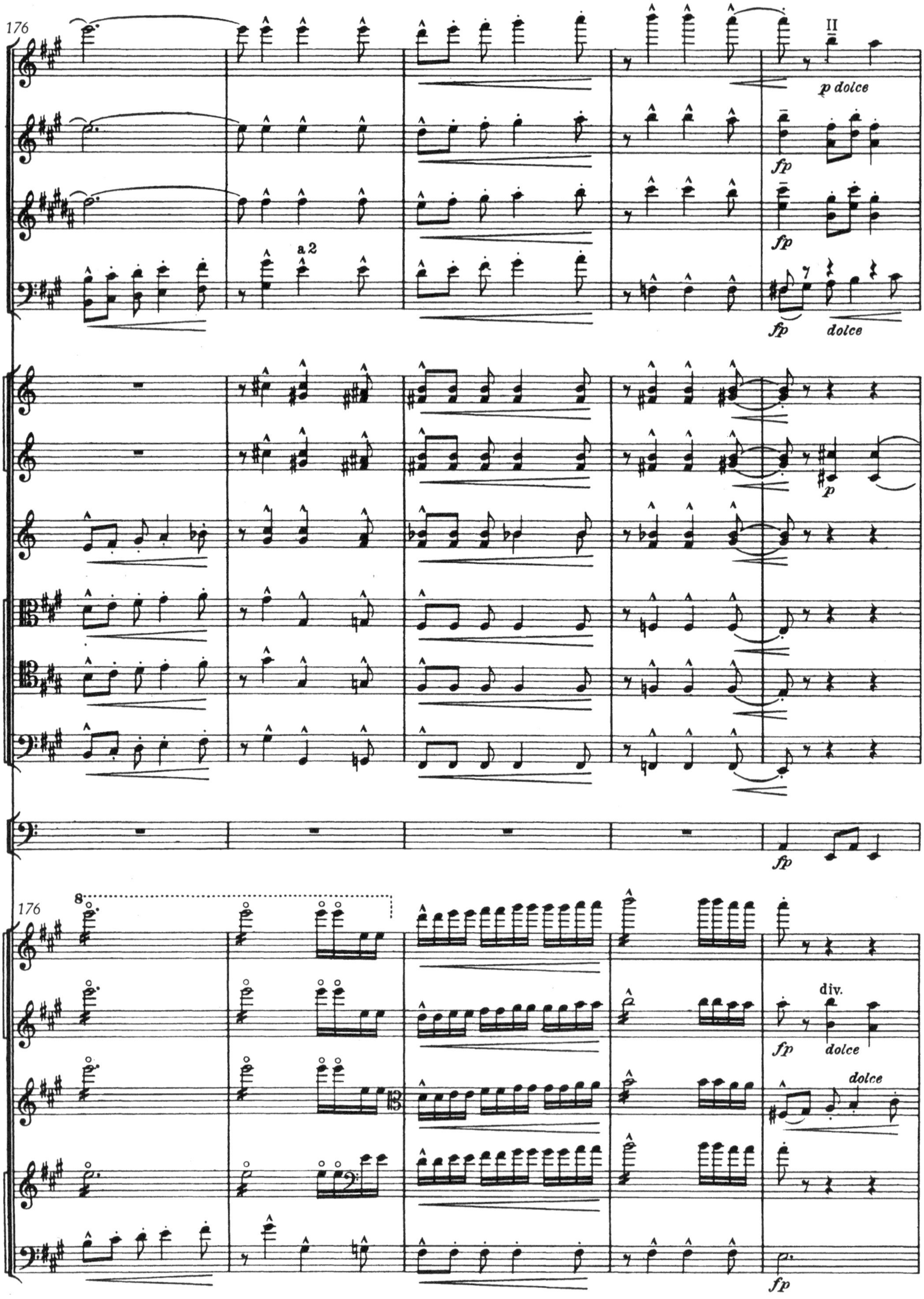
176
II
p dolce
fp
fp
a 2
fp
dolce
fp
176
8
div.
fp
dolce
dolce
fp
fp

181
I
p dolce
cresc. poco a poco
a 2
a 2
cresc. poco a poco
cresc. poco a poco
II
I
cresc. poco a poco
p dolce
cresc. poco a poco
cresc. poco a poco
181
div.
p dolce
cresc. poco a poco
cresc. poco a poco
p dolce
cresc. poco a poco

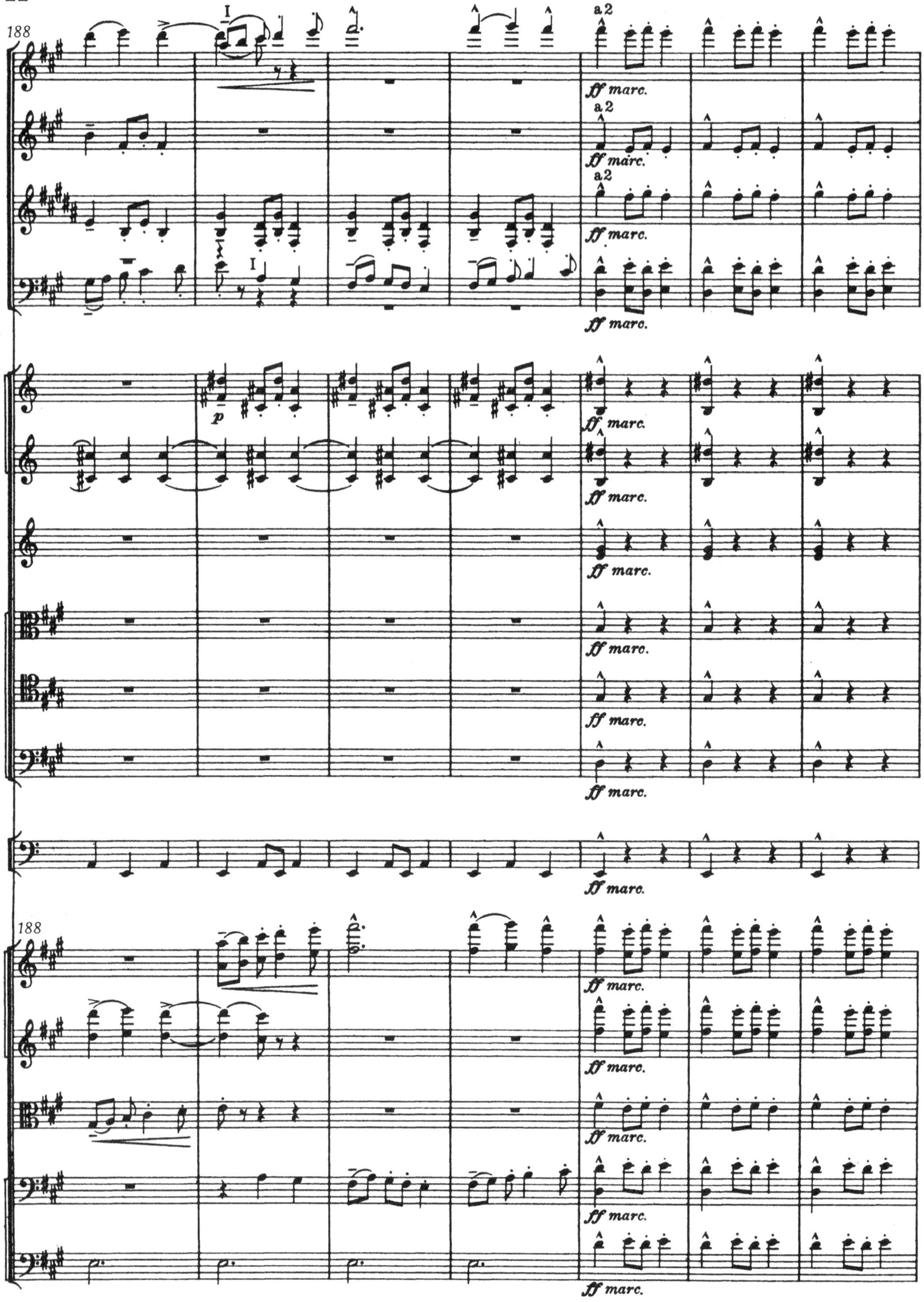
188
I
a 2
ff marc.
p
188

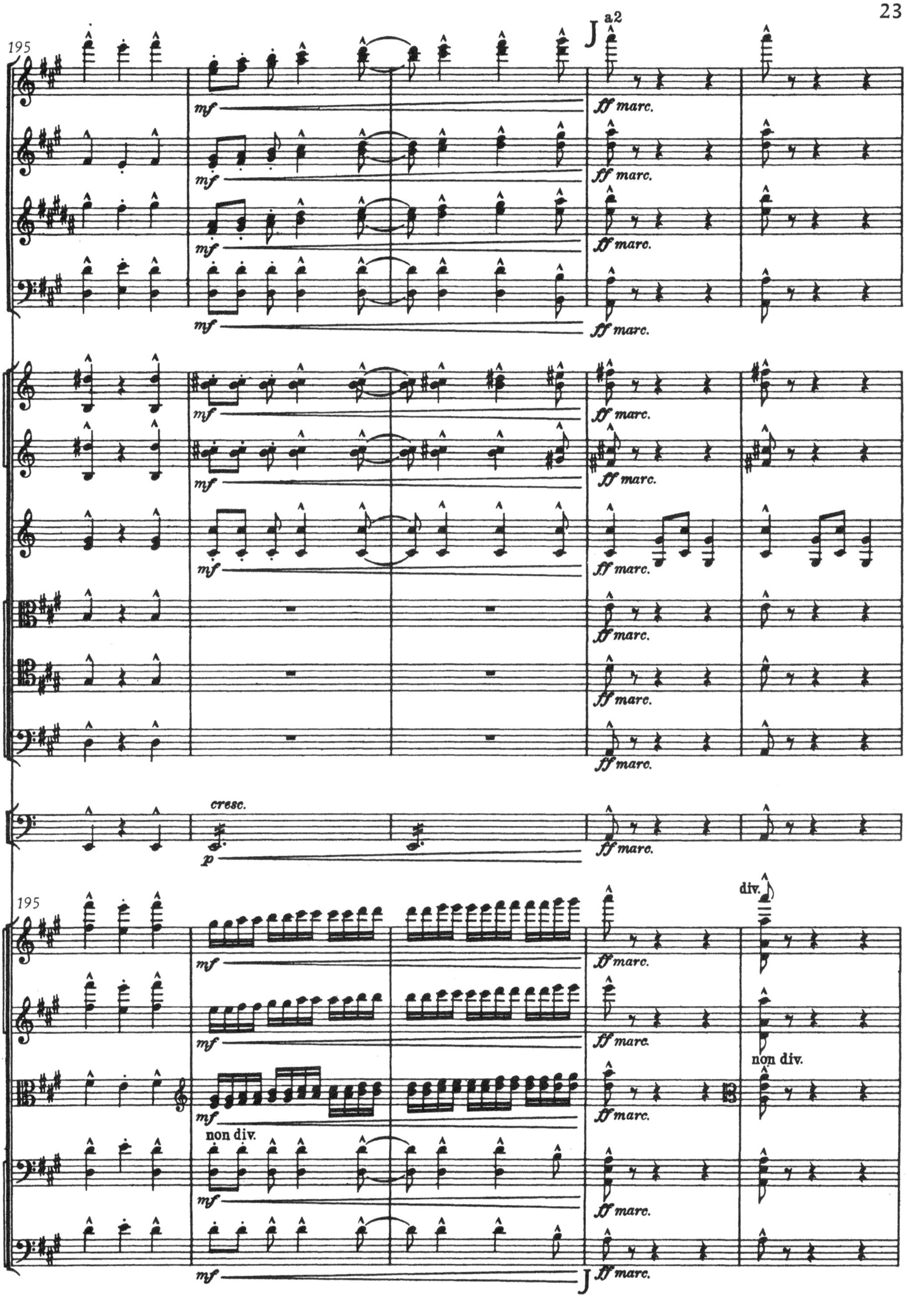
195
J
a2
mf
ff marc.
cresc.
p
div.
non div.

24

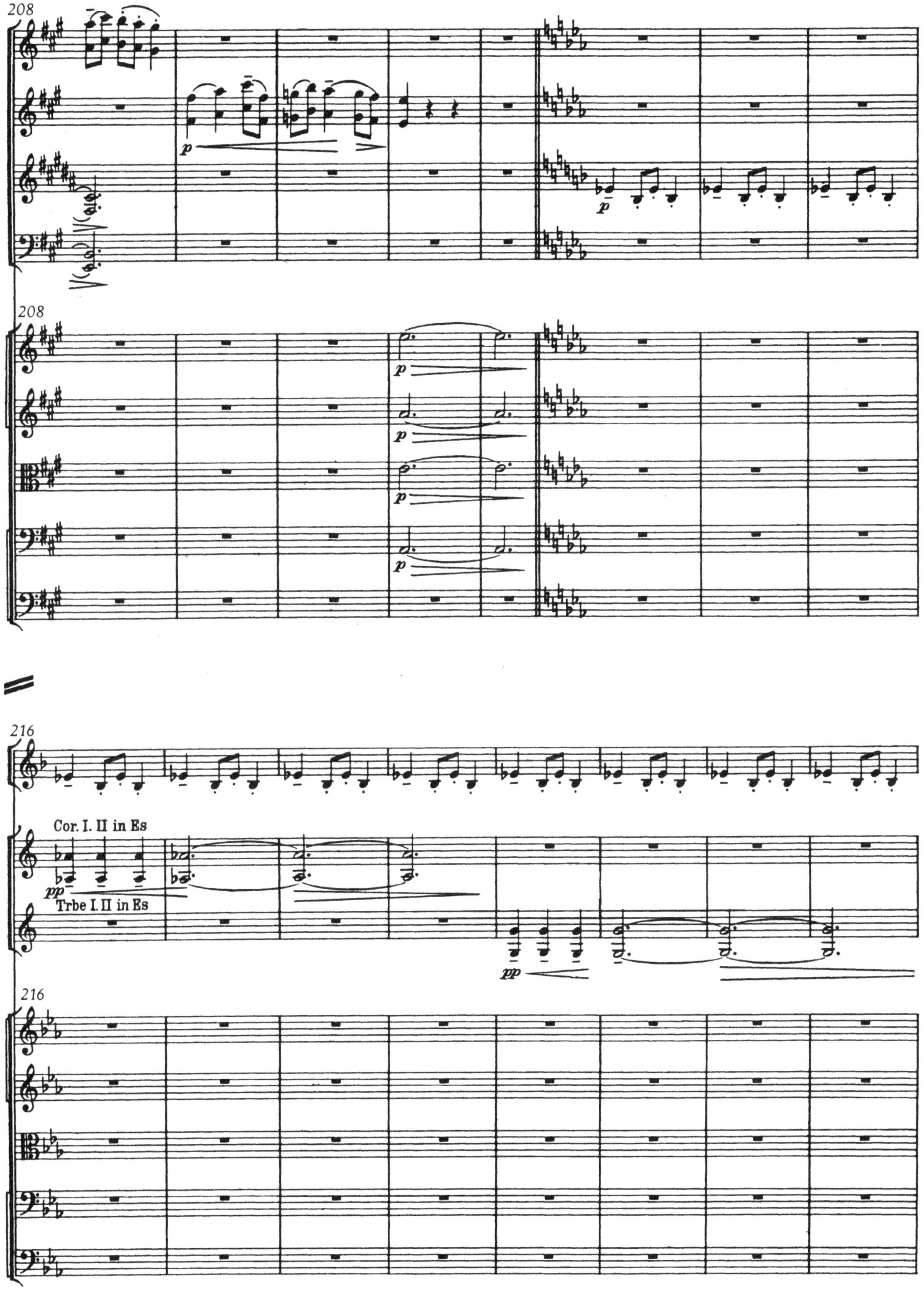
208
p
208
p
p
p
p
216
Cor. I. II in Es
pp
Trbe I. II in Es
pp
216

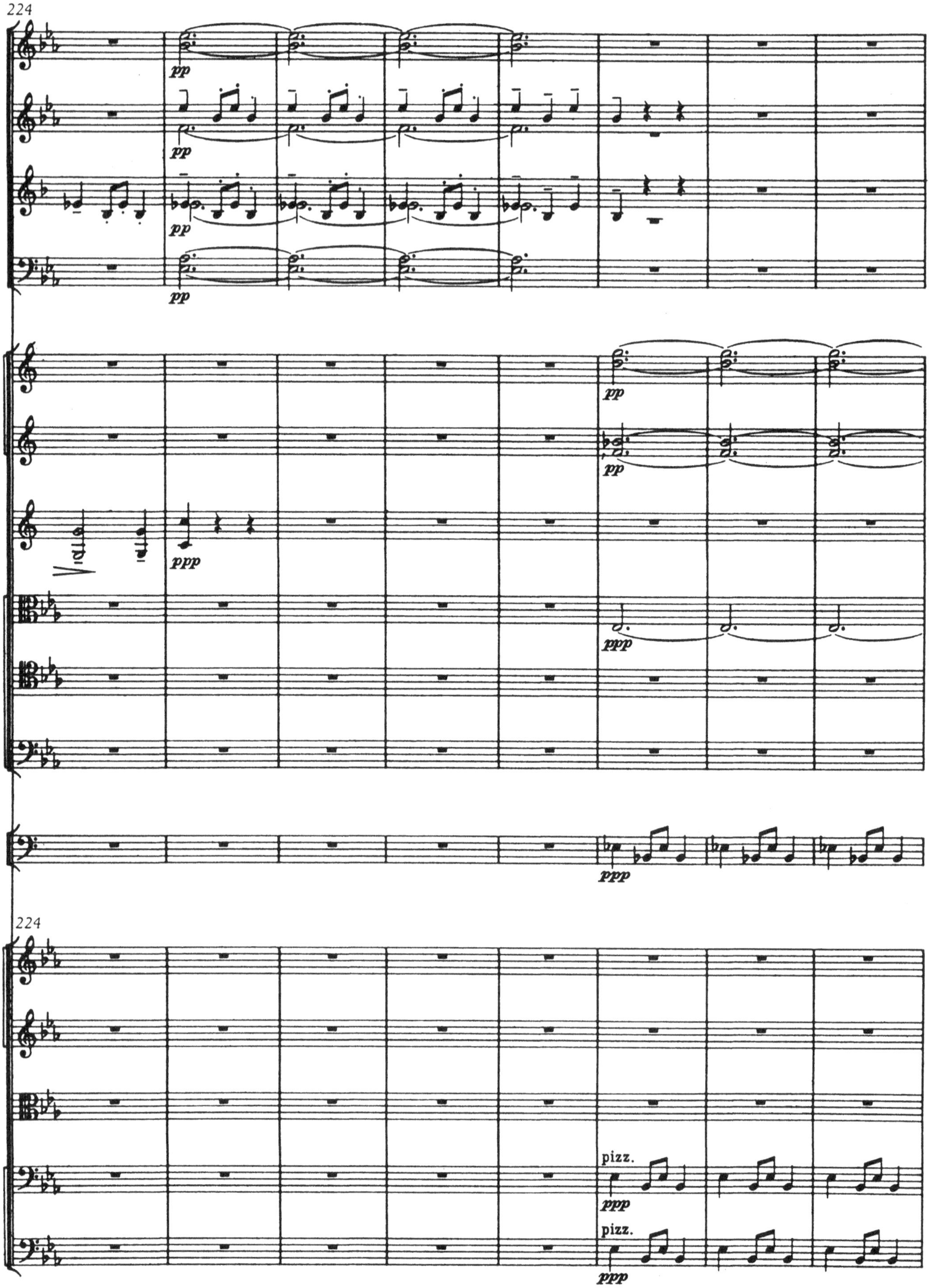
224
pp
pp
pp
pp
pp
pp
ppp
ppp
ppp
224
pizz.
ppp
pizz.
ppp

Tempo I
K
232
pp legg. sempre staccato e legg.
I
pp legg. sempre staccato e legg.
I
p dolce
I
pp
p dolce
legg.
pp
K Tempo I

241
dolce
I
p
Cor. in Es
I
pp
pp
241
legg.
pp
legg.
pp
248
p
248
p
legg.
arco
pp
p

254
a2
cresc. poco a poco
mf
marc.
f
ff
p cresc. poco a poco
a2
f marc.
254
div.
cresc. poco a poco
arco
p

261
a2
f
a2
f
p dim.
I
p dim.
I
p dim.
Cor. I. II in Es
f
p dim.
261
f
f
dim. poco a poco
dim. poco a poco
dim. poco a poco
dim. poco a poco
dim. poco a poco
270
L
p
p
p marc.
pp
pp
pp
pp
I
p marc.
270
div.
pp
pp
pp
pp
pp
L pp

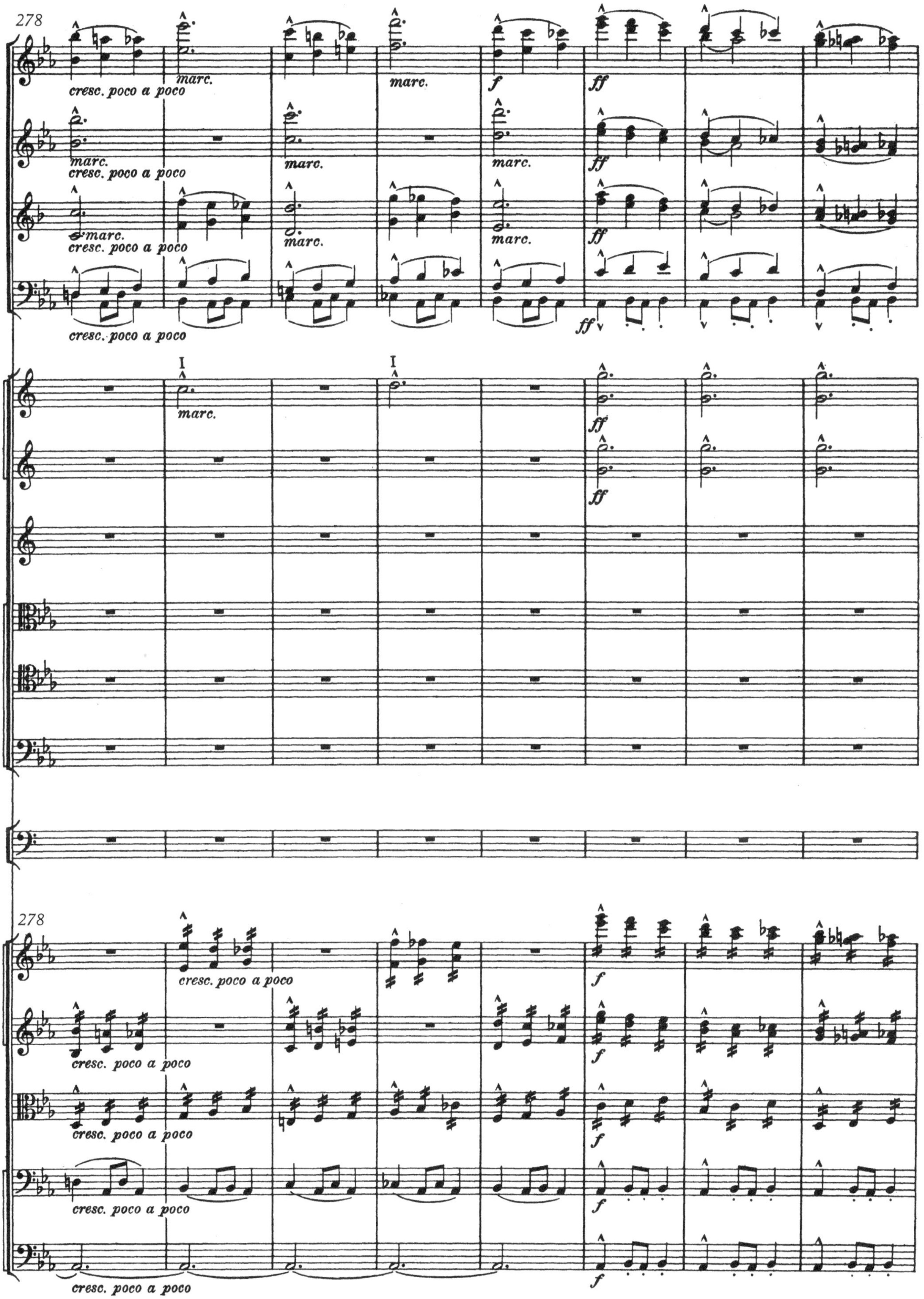
278
cresc. poco a poco
marc.
f
ff
I
278
cresc. poco a poco
f

286
ff
ff
ff
ff
ff
ff
a 2
ff
ff
ff
ff
ff
286
non div.
ff
dim.
unis.
div.
non div.
ff
dim.
ff
dim.
non div.
ff
dim.
ff
dim.

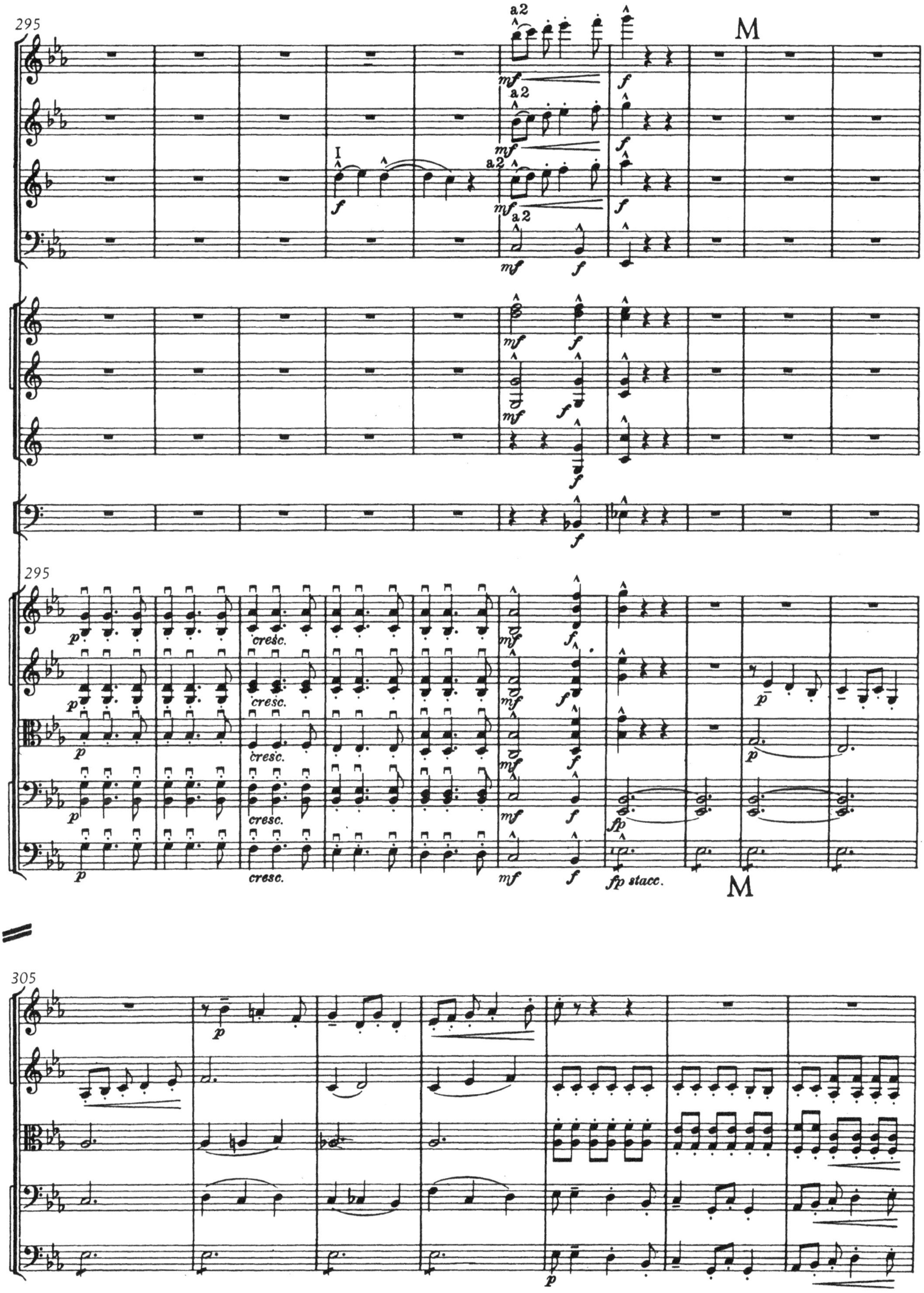
295
a2
M
I
mf
f
295
p
cresc.
fp
fp stacc.
M
305
p

312
Ob.
Clar. in B
Fag.
Cor. in Es
Trbe. in Es
Timp.
I Solo
I Solo
div. pizz.
pizz.
legg. e spiccato assai
legg. e spiccato assai
legg. e spiccato assai
318
Fl.
I
I
a 2
a 2
arco
arco
cresc. poco a poco
cresc. poco a poco
cresc. poco a poco
cresc. poco a poco

324
II Solo
I Solo
f
p
dim.
mf
Trbe in Es
Trbni.
324
pizz.
pizz.
pizz.
pizz.
pizz.

330
mf
mf
cresc. poco a poco
mf
cresc. poco a poco
mf
cresc. poco a poco
330
arco
p
mf
arco
p
mf
arco
p
mf
arco
p
mf
arco
mf

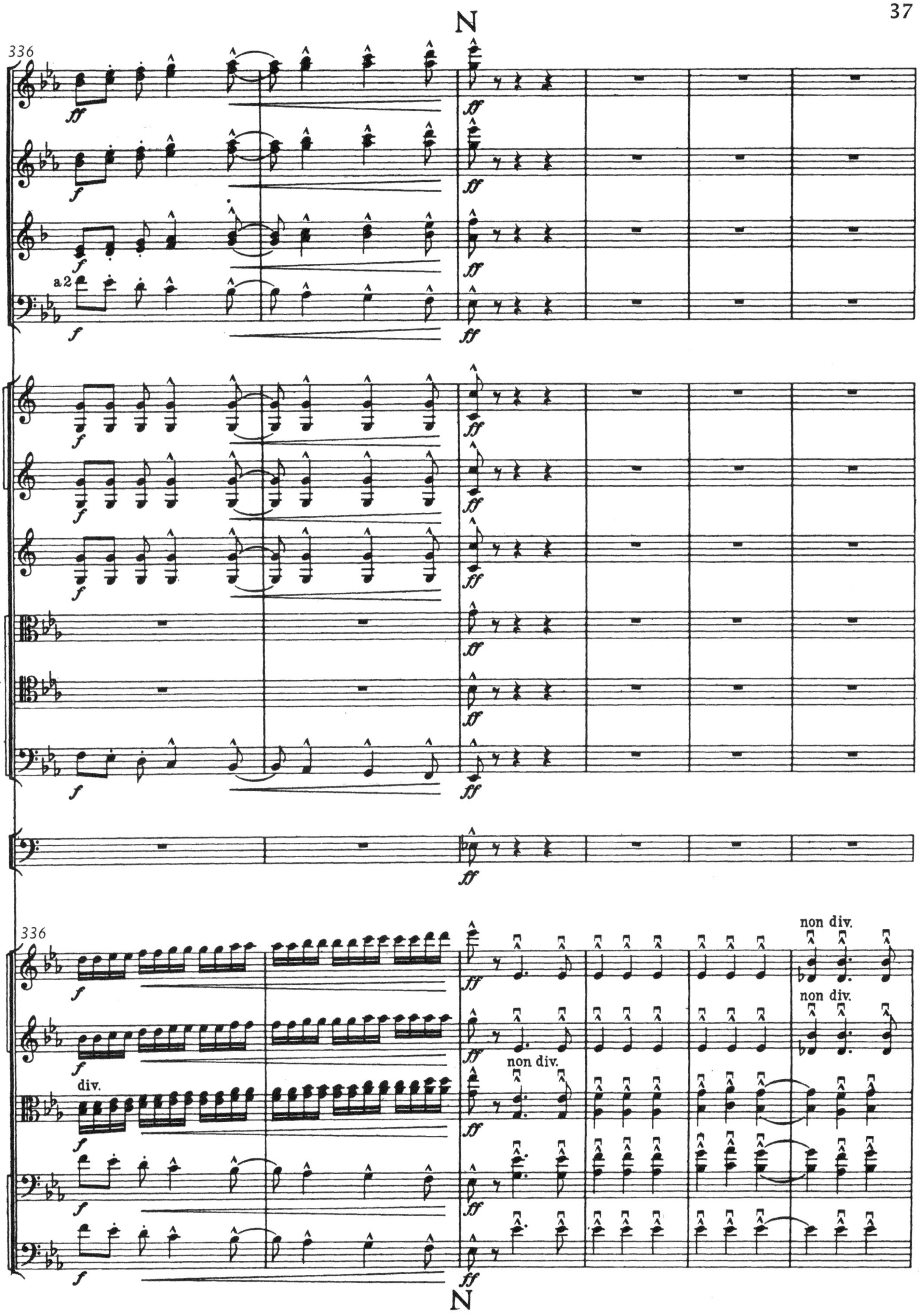
N
336
a2
ff
f
div.
non div.
N

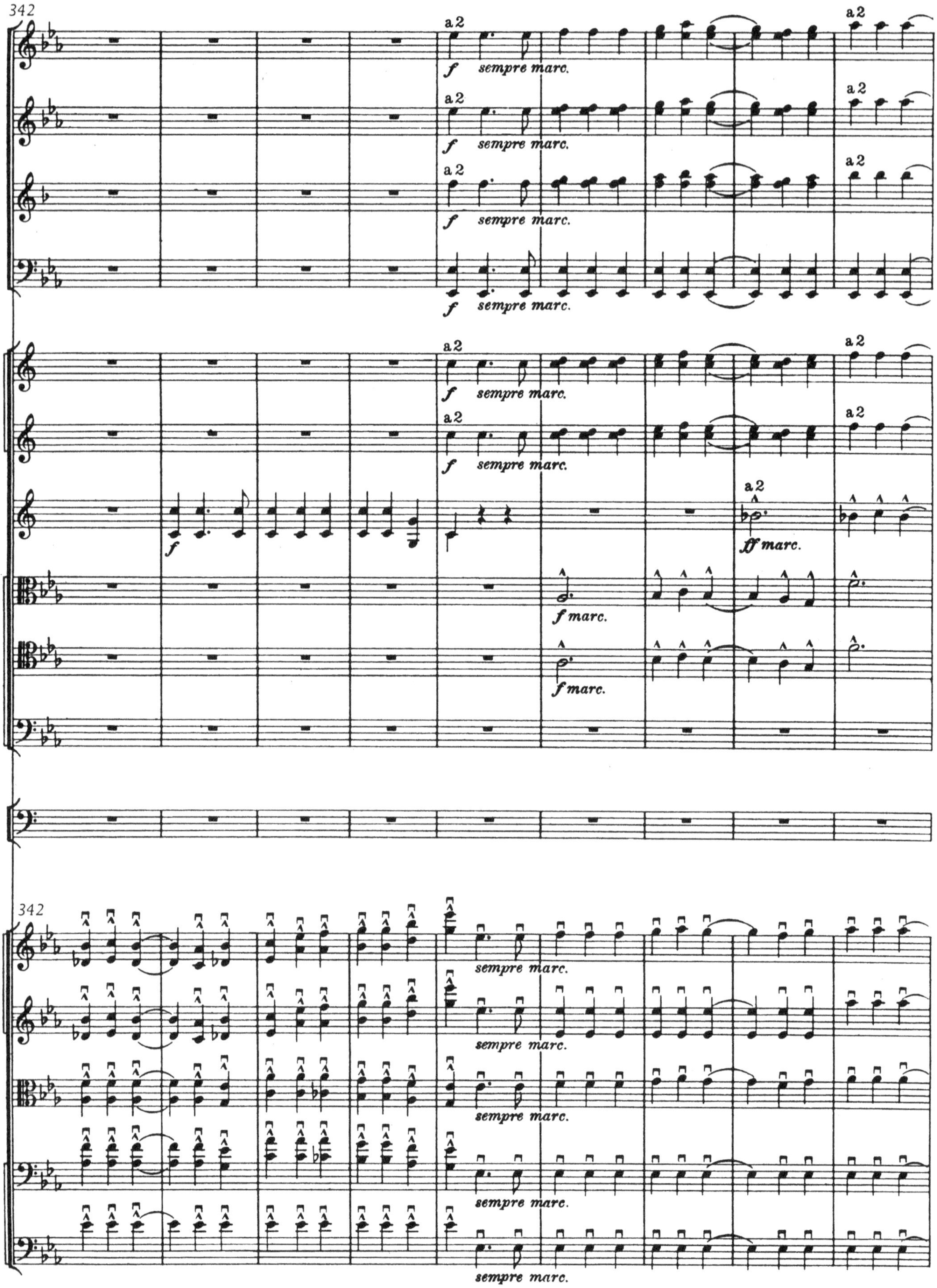
342
a2
f
sempre marc.
f marc.
a2
ff marc.
342
sempre marc.

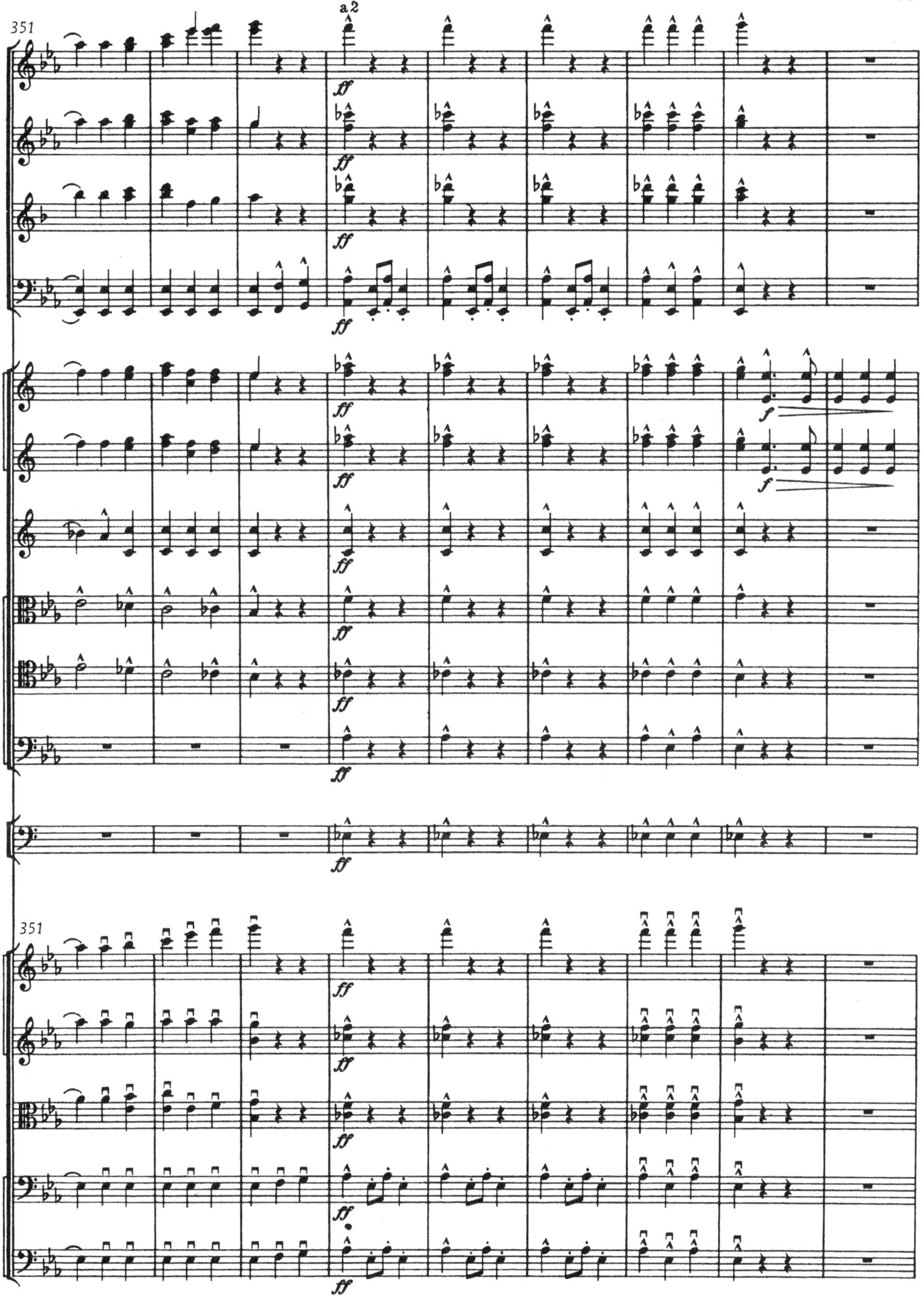
351
a2
ff
f
351
ff

360
p
p
360
p dolce
fp
p dolce
fp
p dolce
p
fp
p dolce
p
fp
p dolce
dim.
dim.
dim.
dim.
dim.
369
Fl.
p
dim.
p
dim.
p
dim.
pp
369
pp
pp
pp
pp
pp
pp
pp

O
378
378
p dolce
p dolce
p dolce
p dolce
O
385
P
p dolce
Ob.
p dolce
a 2
mf marc.
p dolce
a 2
mf marc.
p dolce
385
mf marc.
P

393
Cor. I. II in Es
a 2
f marc.
393
mf marc.
div.
mf marc.
f marc. sempre
f marc. sempre
400
Cor. III. IV in Es
Trbe in Es
a 2
400

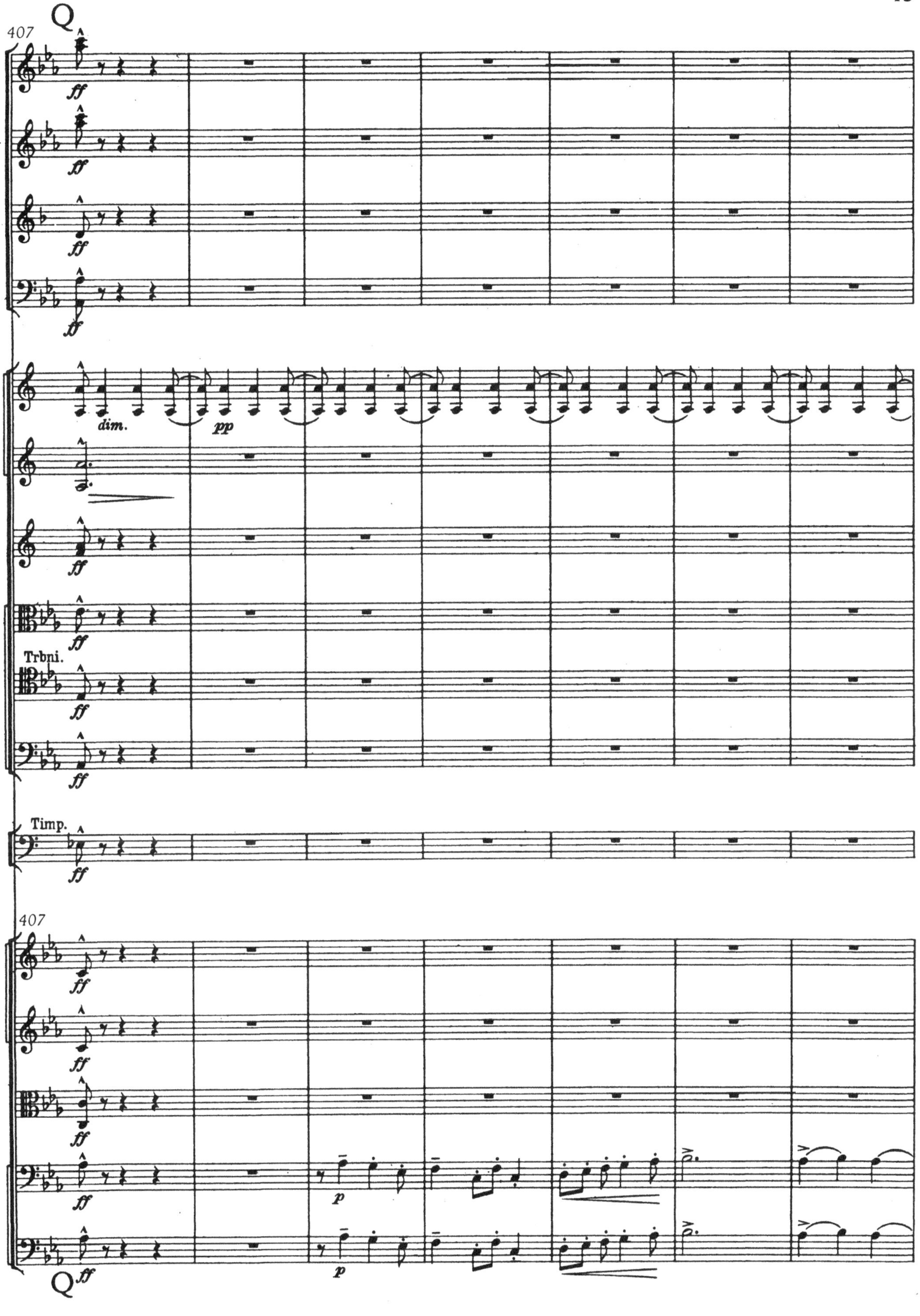
Q
407
ff
dim.
pp
Trbni.
Timp.
p

414
Ob.
I
p
pII
I Solo
I
414
421
Fl.
I Solo
Clar. in B
421
pizz.
pp
pizz.
pp

428
Cor. III in Es
III Solo
pp
Trbe in Es
I Solo
pp
dim.
ppp
428
435
Clar. in B
p
Fag.
p
dim.
ppp
435

442
dim.
442
449
R
a2
a 2
Ob.
a 2
fp
f
p
fp dolce
Timp.
449
p dolce
fp dolce
arco
div.
fp
R

457
Clar. in B
p
cresc. poco a poco
cresc. poco a poco
I
cresc. poco a poco
cresc. poco a poco
Trbe in Es
Trbni
cresc. poco a poco
457
p dolce
cresc.
cresc. poco a poco
cresc. poco a poco
arco
p dolce
cresc. poco a poco
cresc. poco a poco

48

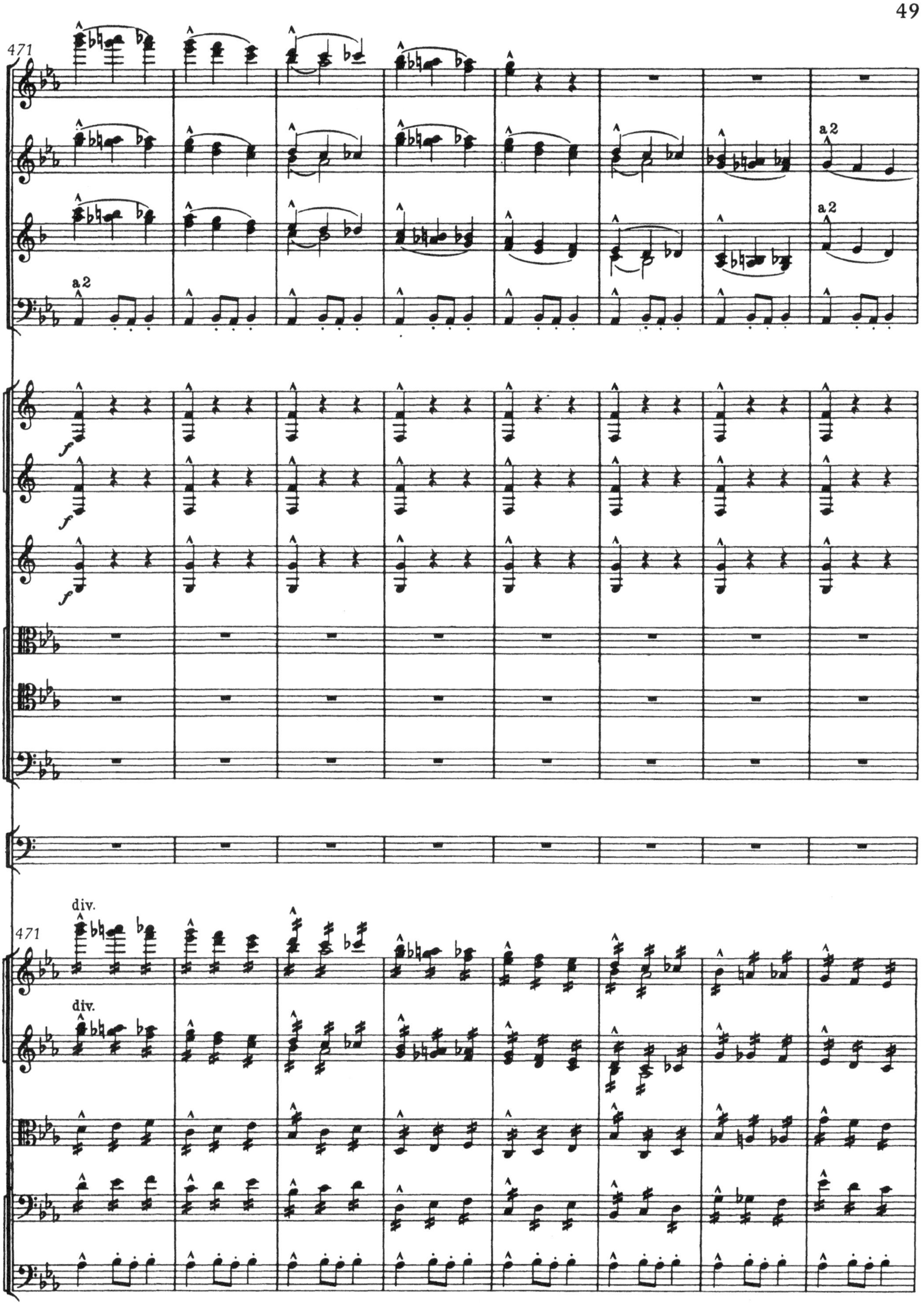
471
a 2
a 2
a 2
f
f
f
div.
div.
471

479
poco a poco più animato
a2
S Animato assai
ff marc.
479
poco a poco più animato
S Animato assai

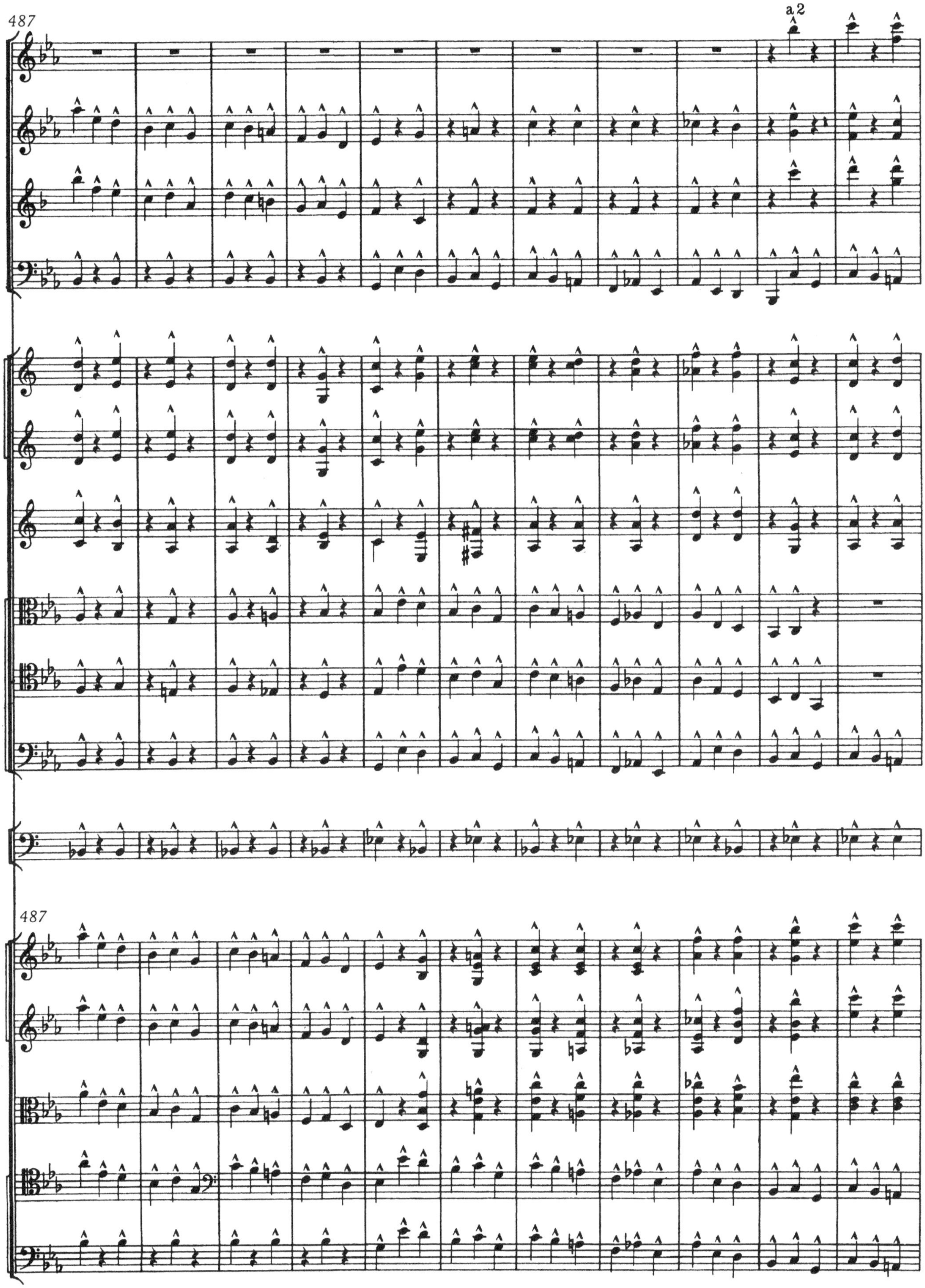
487
a 2
487

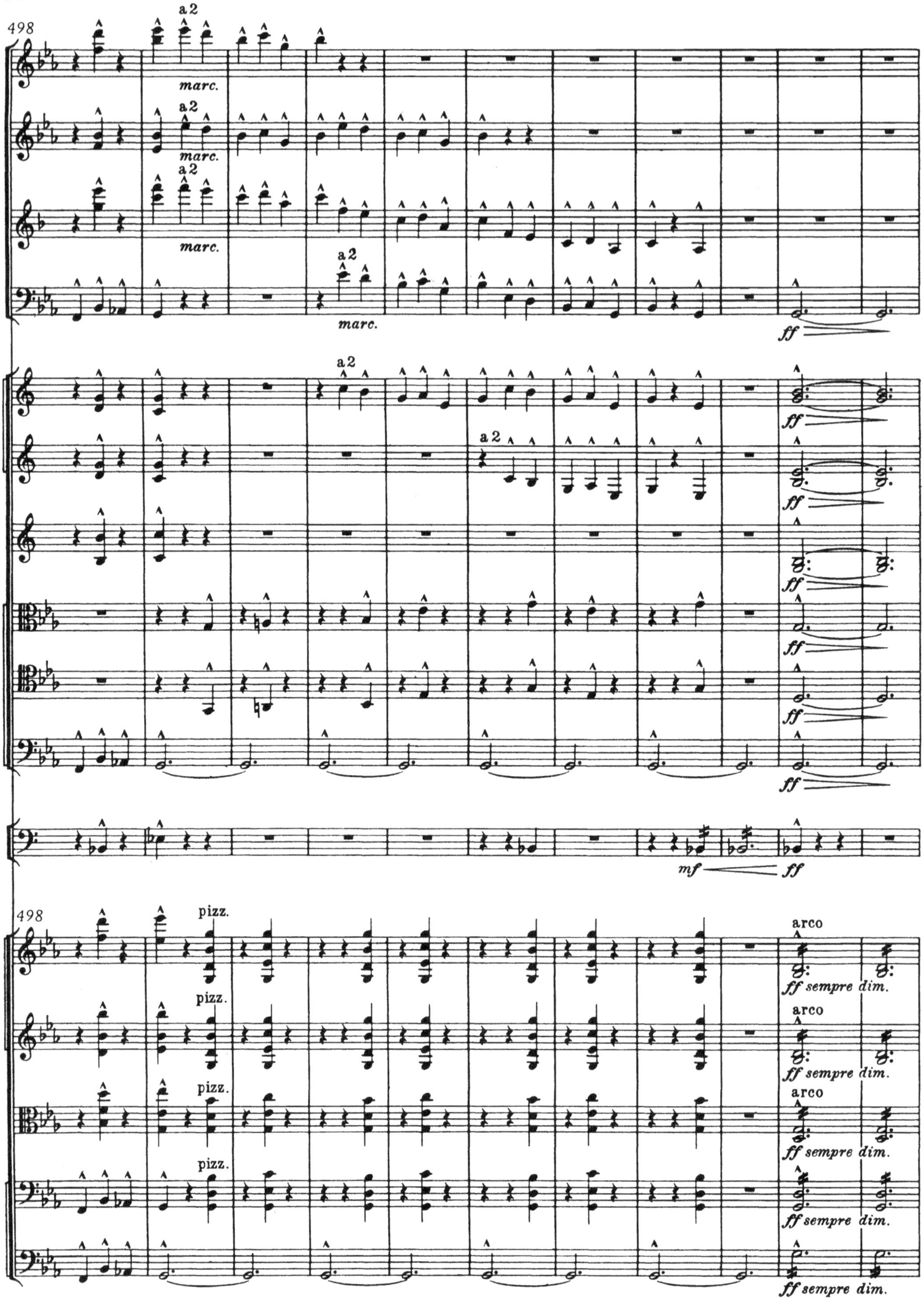
498
a 2
marc.
pizz.
arco
ff
mf
ff sempre dim.

509
Andantino 𝅗𝅥 = 92
I Solo
p dolce
Cor. I in Es
p dolce
509
div.
dim.
ppp
p dolce
Andantino 𝅗𝅥 = 92
517
a 2
a 2
517
div.
div.
a 2

523
Fl.
T
p
a 2
523
con sord.
p
con sord.
con sord.
T
529
I
p dolce
II
a 2
mf
Cor. I. II in Es
pp
529
div.
p

535
pp
pp
ppp
pizz.
pp
541
Ob.
mf dim.
p morendo
pp
ppp
mf dim.
p
mf dim.
p morendo
pp
ppp
mf dim.
mf dim.
mf dim.
541
pp
pizz.
pp
pizz.
pp
pizz.
pp
pizz.
pp
pizz.
pp

56

II
SCHERZO

20
A
p
p legg.
pp legg.
pp
Timp.
pizz.
30
cresc.
mf
I Solo
Cor. in Es
non div.
arco
fp

40
I
II
p
40
arco
p
arco
p
49
a 2
mf
a 2
mf
a 2
mf
p
II
mf
pp
49
mf
mf
mf
arco
mf

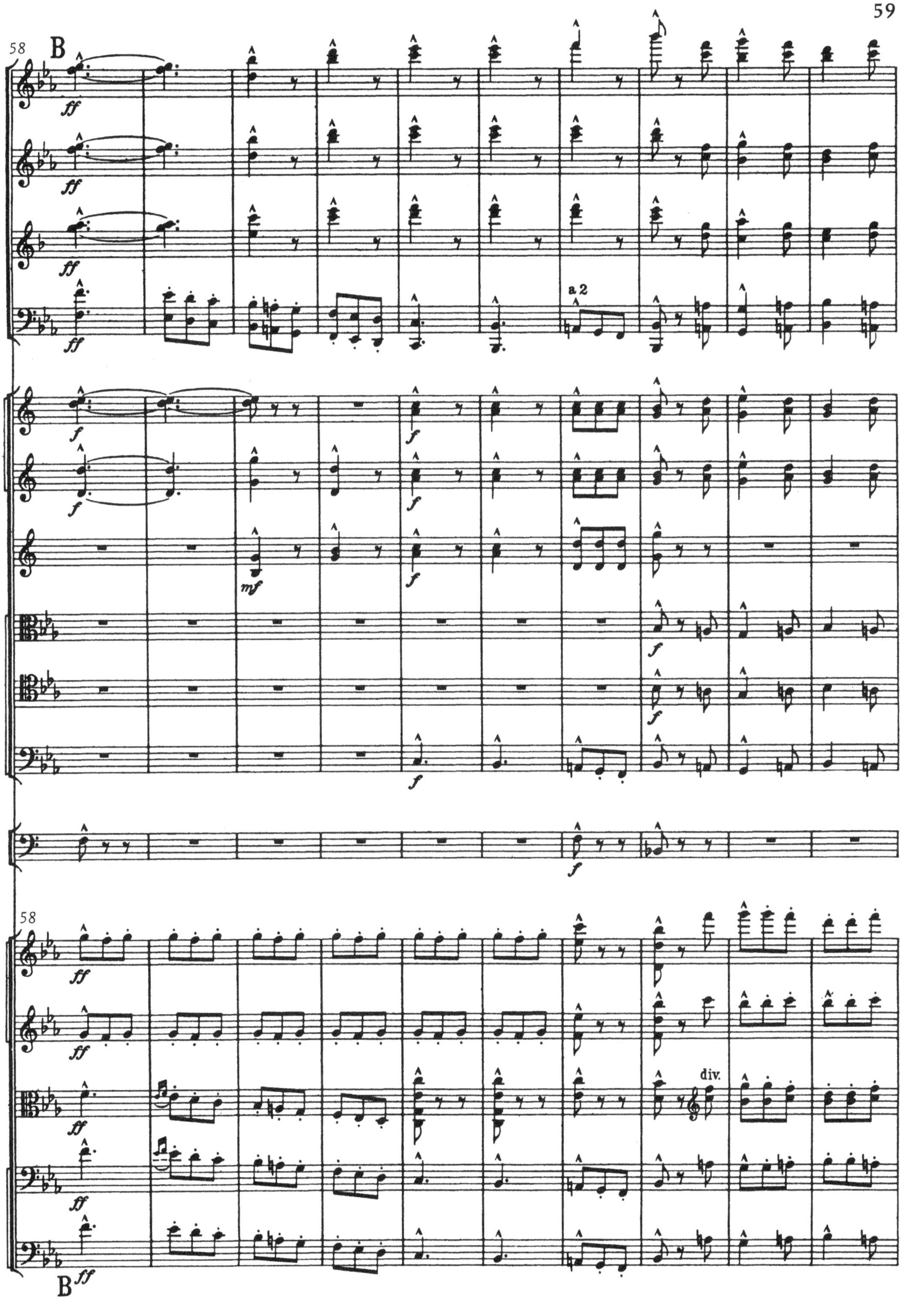
58
B
ff
a 2
f
mf
div.
B

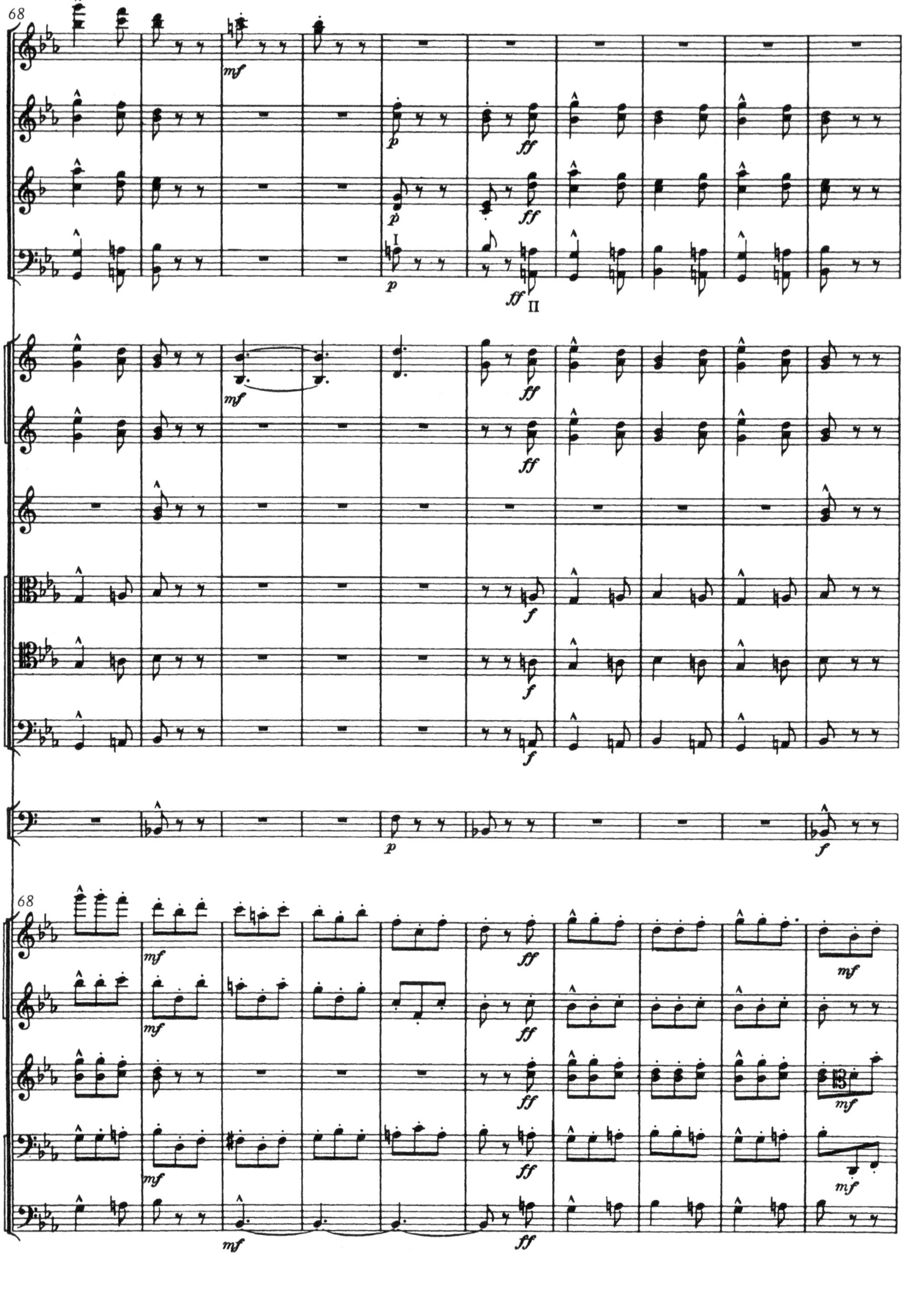
68
mf
p
ff
I
II
f
68
mf

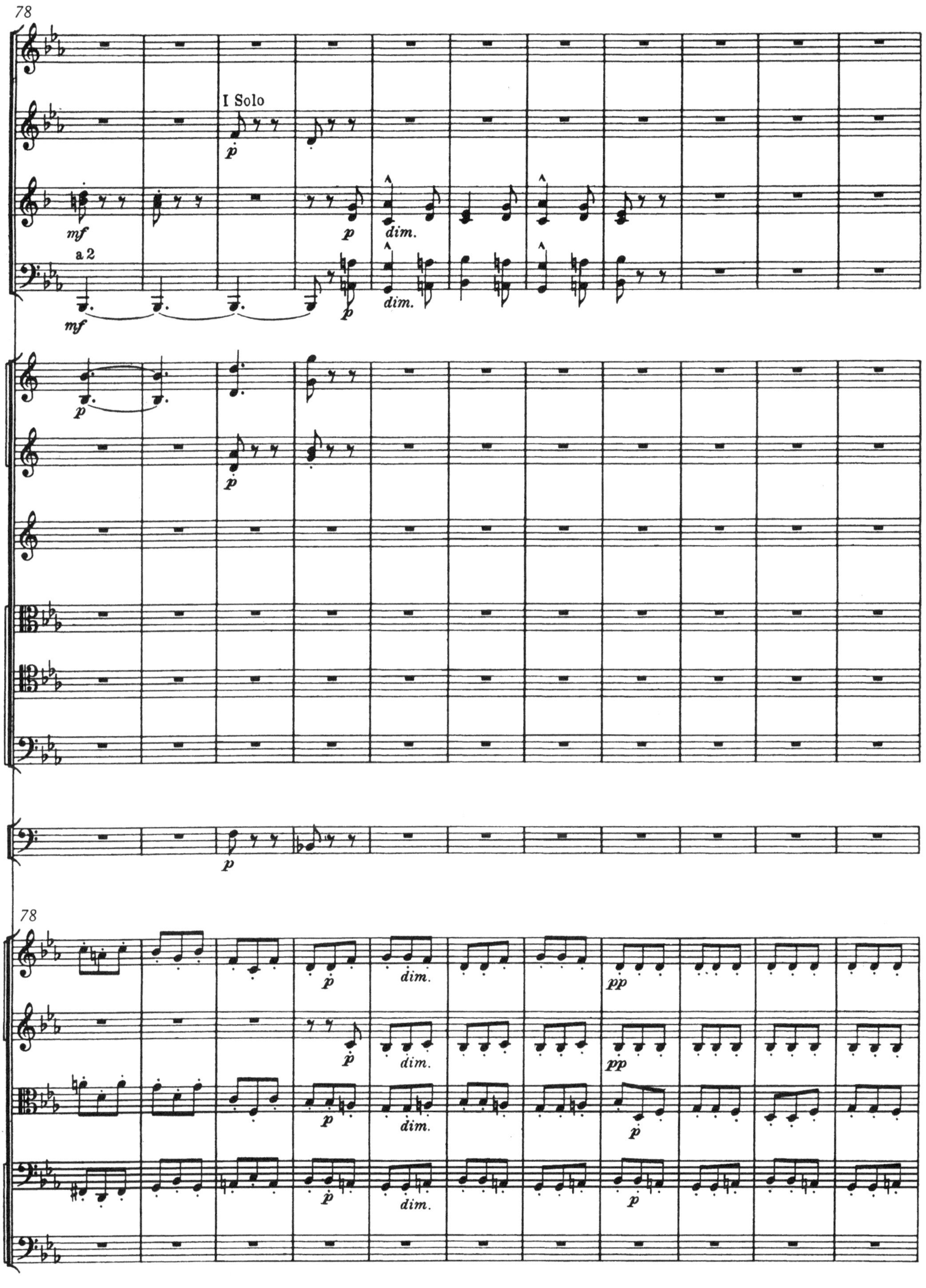
78
I Solo
p
mf
p
dim.
a 2
mf
p
dim.
p
p
p
78
p
dim.
pp
p
dim.
pp
p
dim.
p
p
dim.
p

62

101
C
a 2
p marc.
a 2
p cresc.
marc.
Cor. I. II in Es
a 2
p cresc.
101
p cresc.
cresc. poco a poco
p cresc.
pizz.
cresc. poco a poco
p
pizz.
p
C
111
f
f
f
Fag.
a 2
f
f
marc.
mf
p
111
f
f dim.
p
p
arco
f dim.
f
arco
pizz.
p
f dim.
p

121
Ob.
ff marc.
ff marc.
fp I
121
p
p
div
div.
p cresc.
pizz.
p
p
130
Fl.
ff marc.
a2
a2
a2
ff
dim.
ff
Trbe in Es
mf
dim.
p
p
130
ff marc.
ff marc.
dim.
f
f
dim.
f

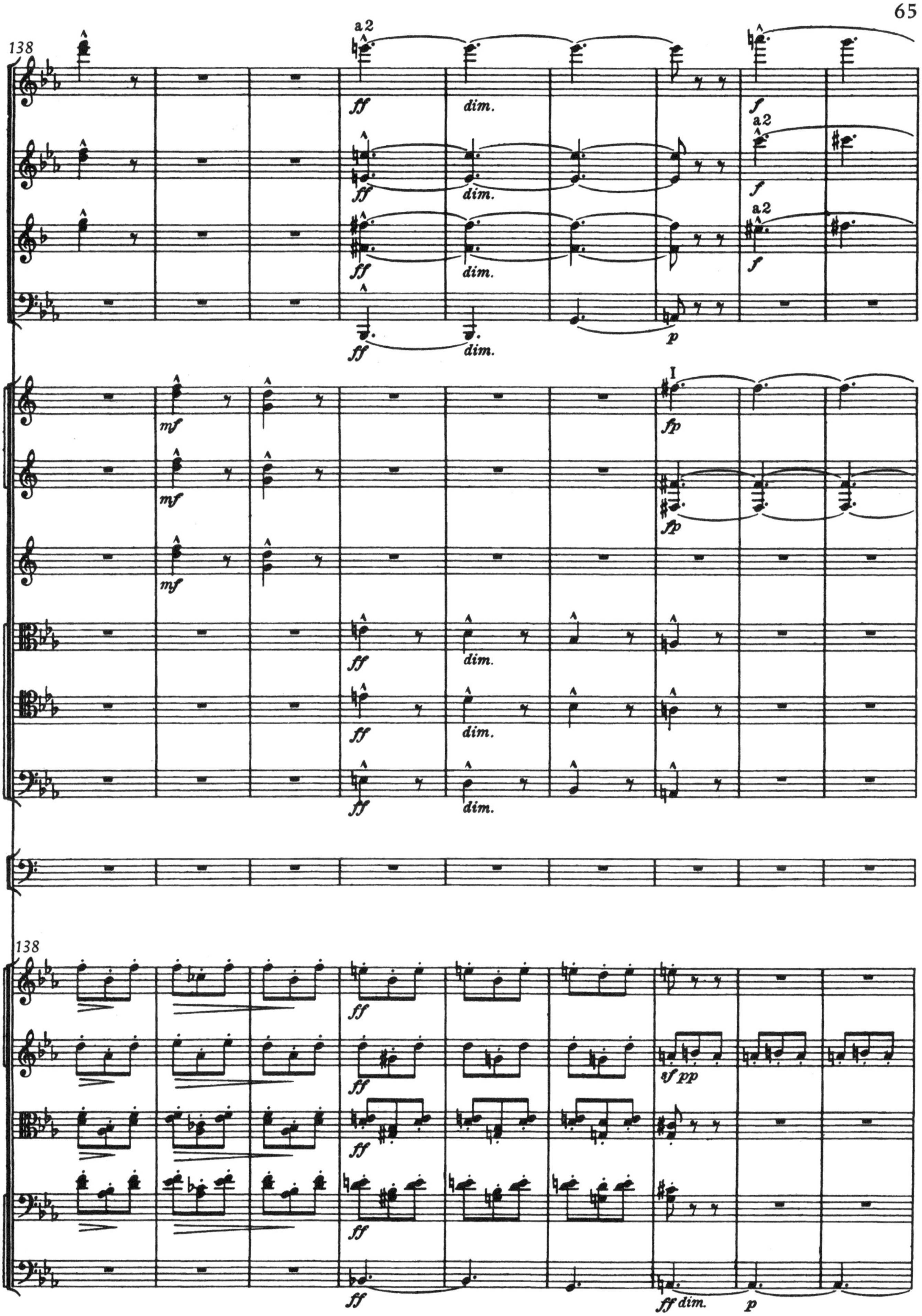
138
a2
ff
dim.
p
f
a2
I
mf
fp
138
sf pp
ff dim.

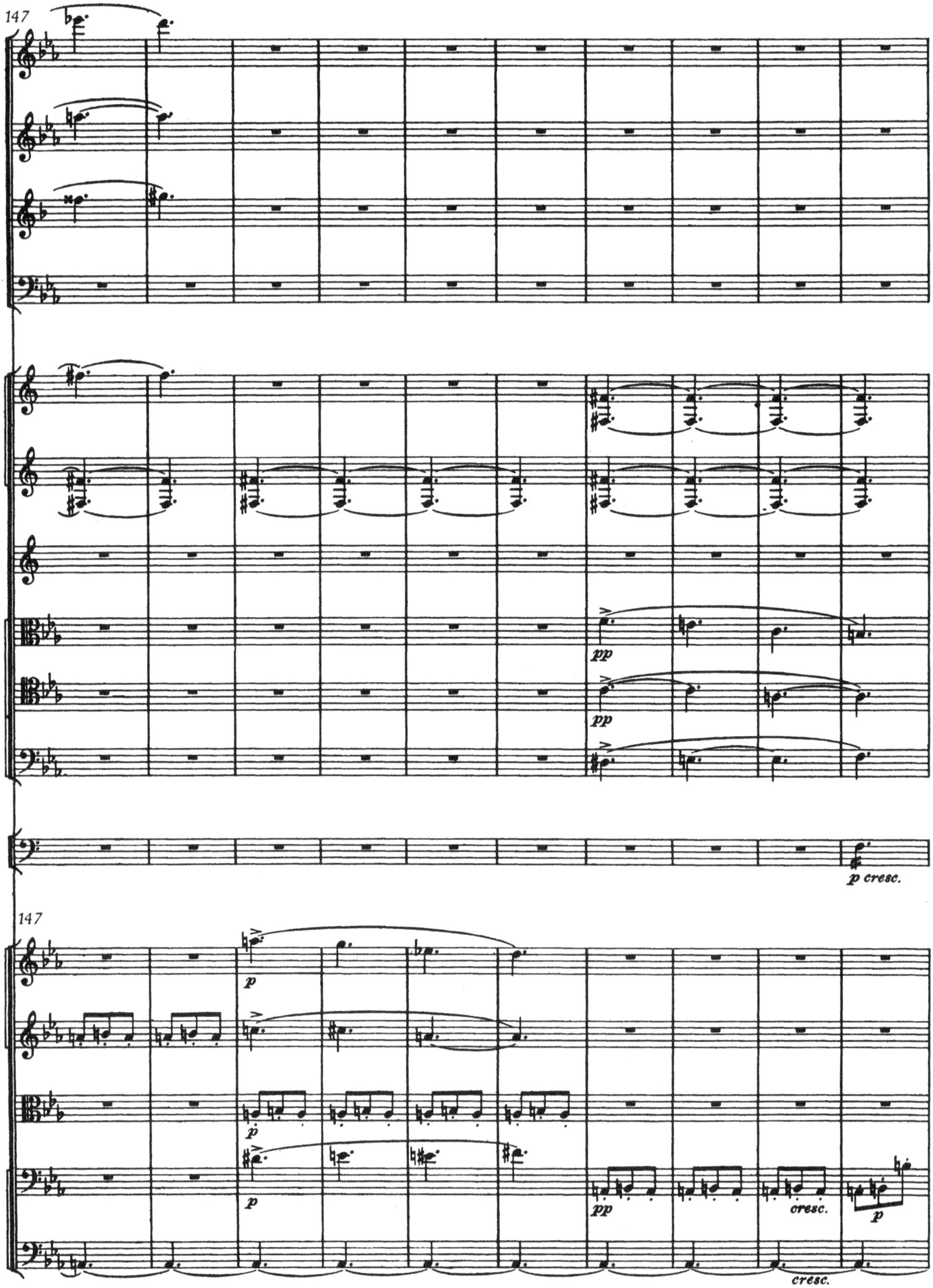
147
pp
pp
p cresc.
147
p
p
p
pp
cresc.
p
cresc.

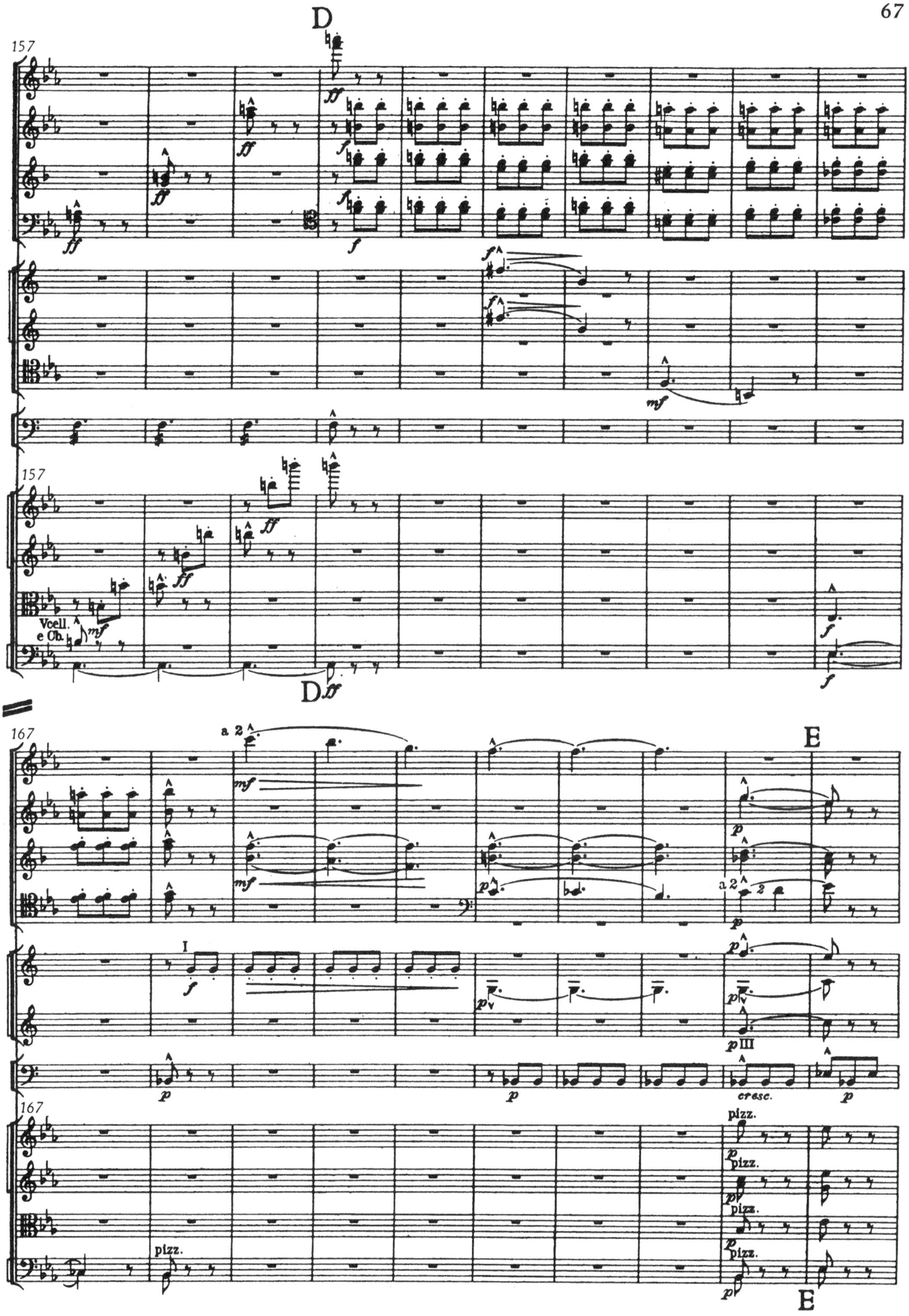
D
157
ff
f
157
Vcell. e Cb.
mf
ff
D
167
a 2
E
mf
p
I
f
p III
cresc.
pizz.
E

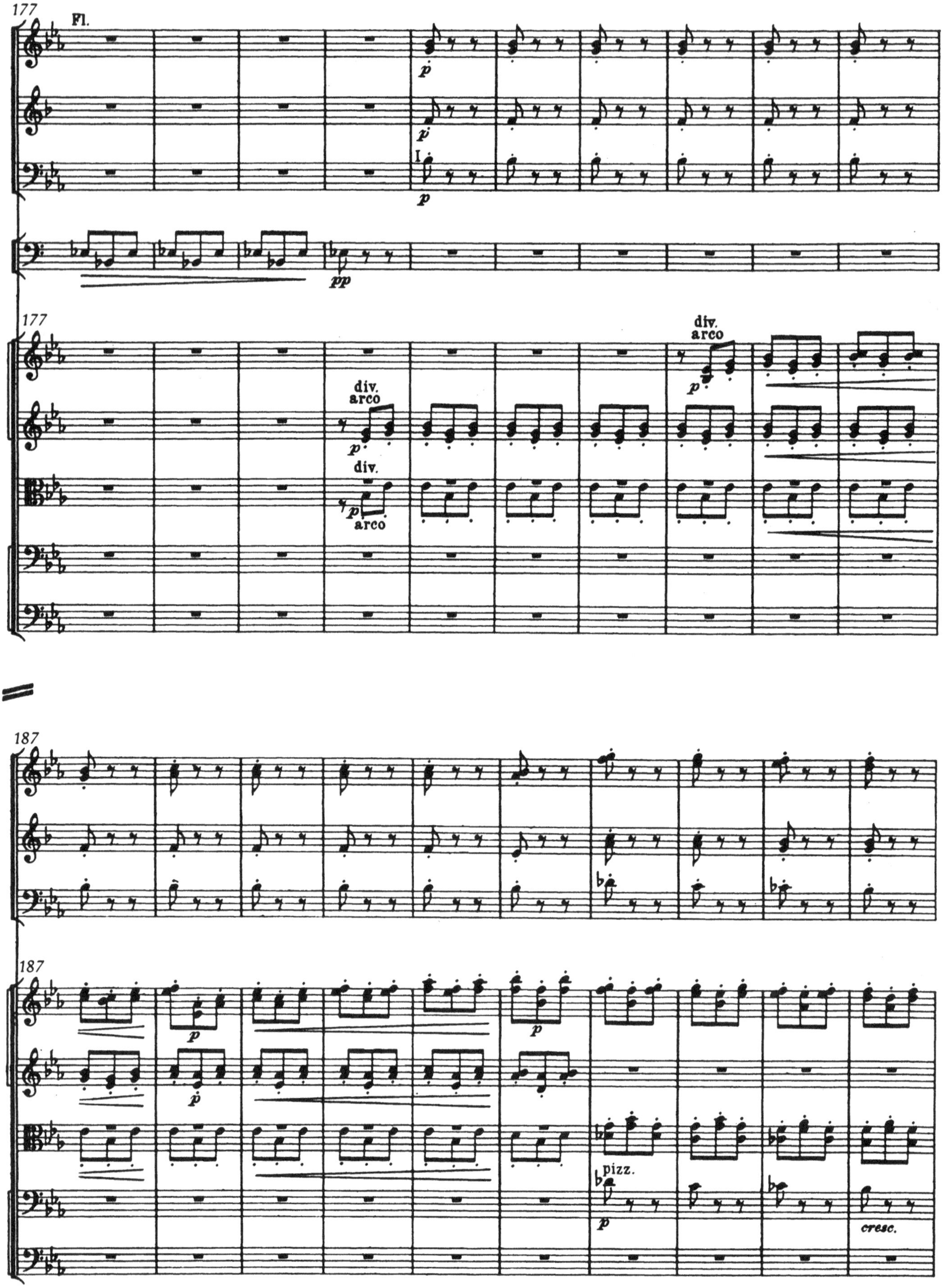
177
Fl.
I
p
pp
177
div.
arco
div.
arco
div.
arco
187
187
pizz.
cresc.

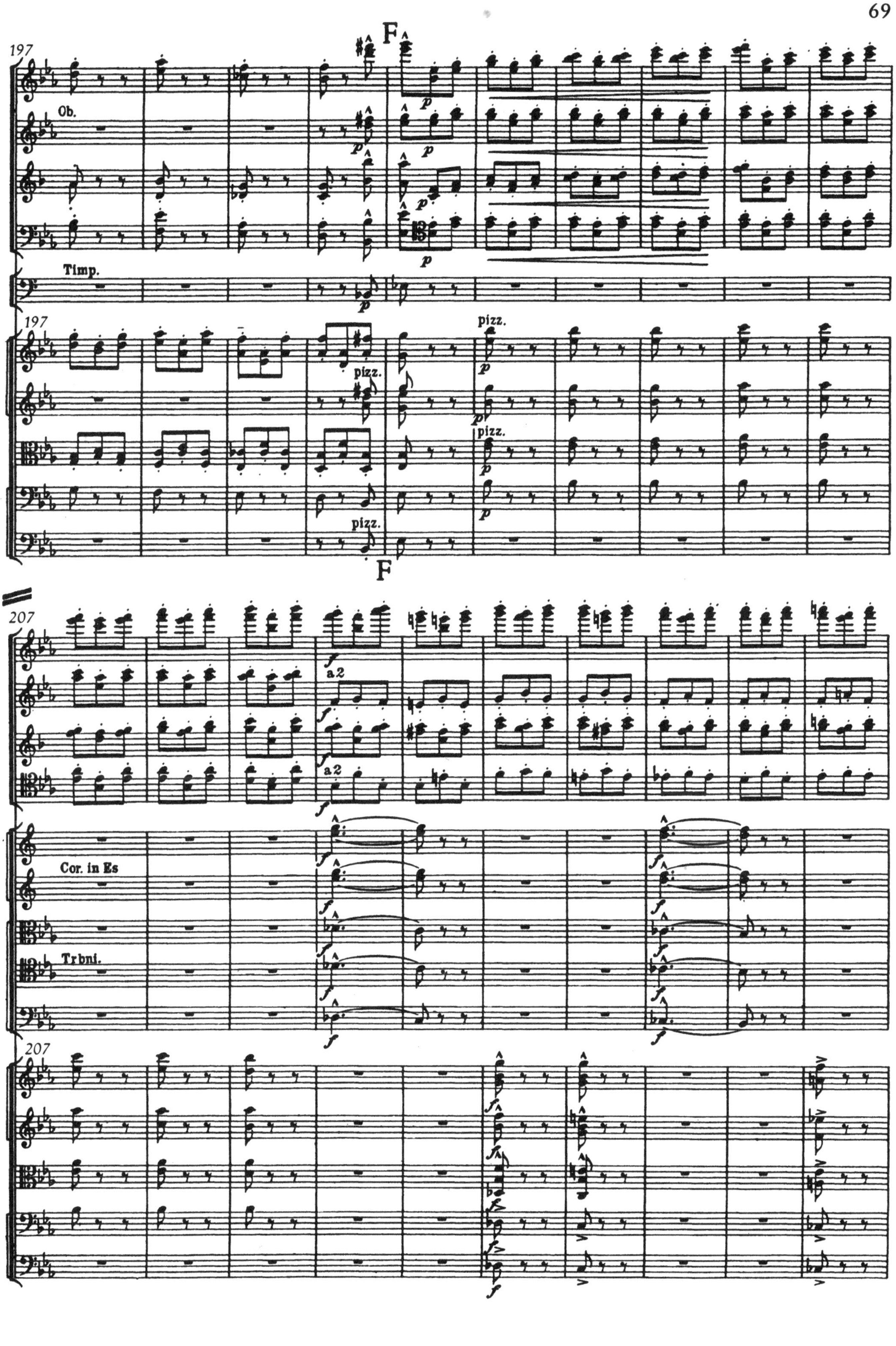
197
F
Ob.
Timp.
pizz.
207
a 2
Cor. in Es
Trbni.

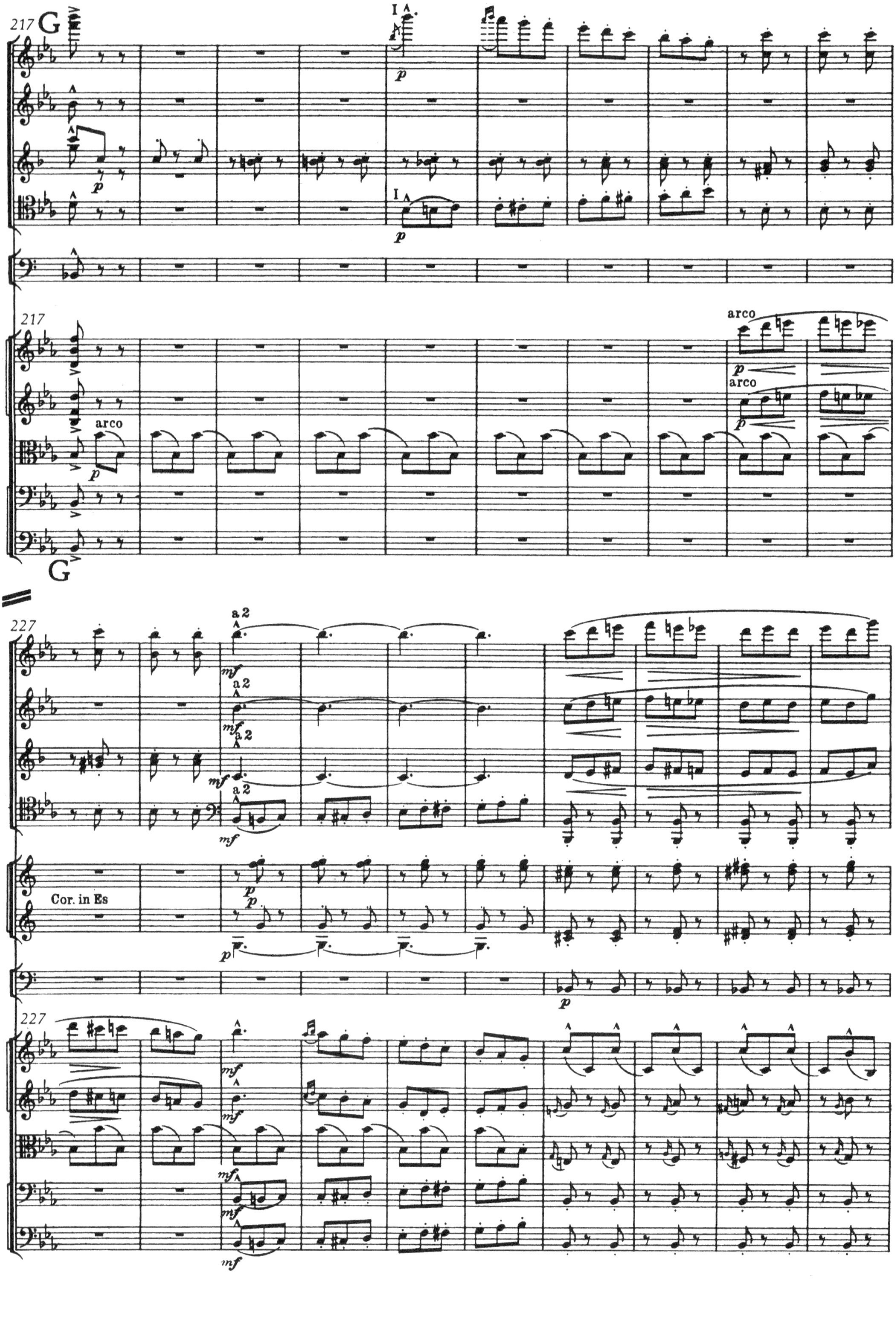
217 G
I
arco
G
227
a 2
Cor. in Es
mf
p

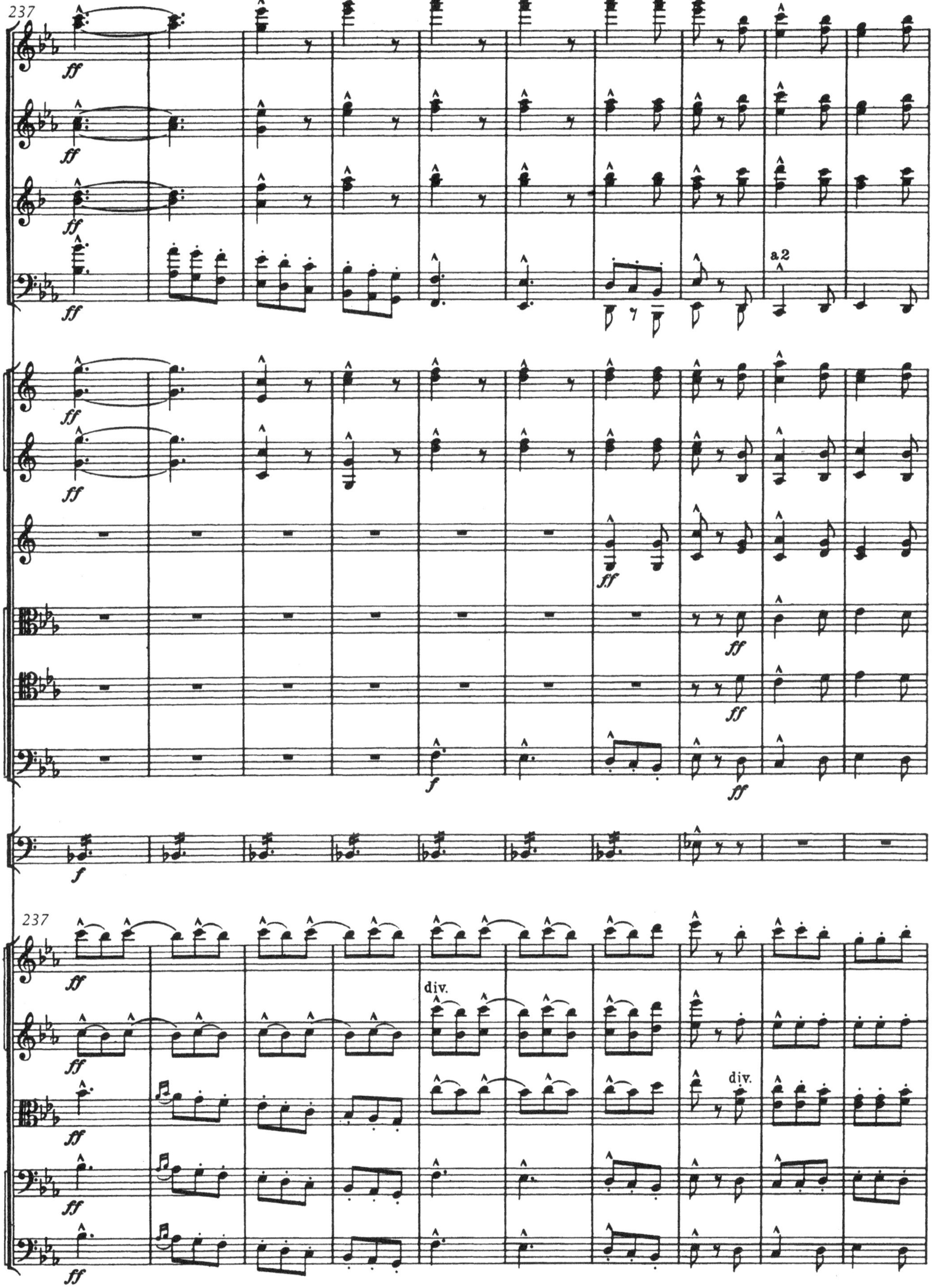
237
ff
a 2
f
div.

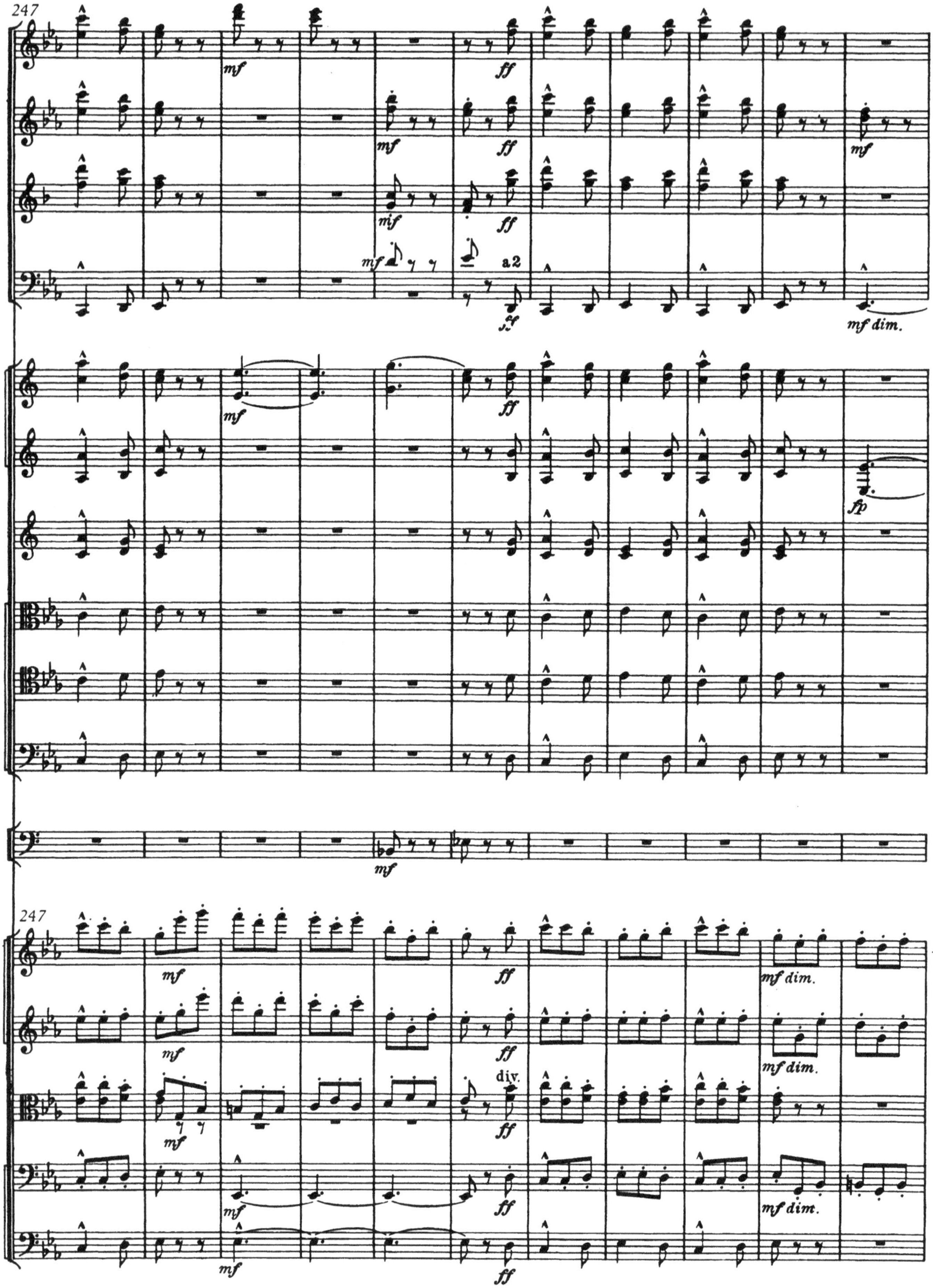
247
mf
ff
mf dim.
a2
fp
div.
mf dim.

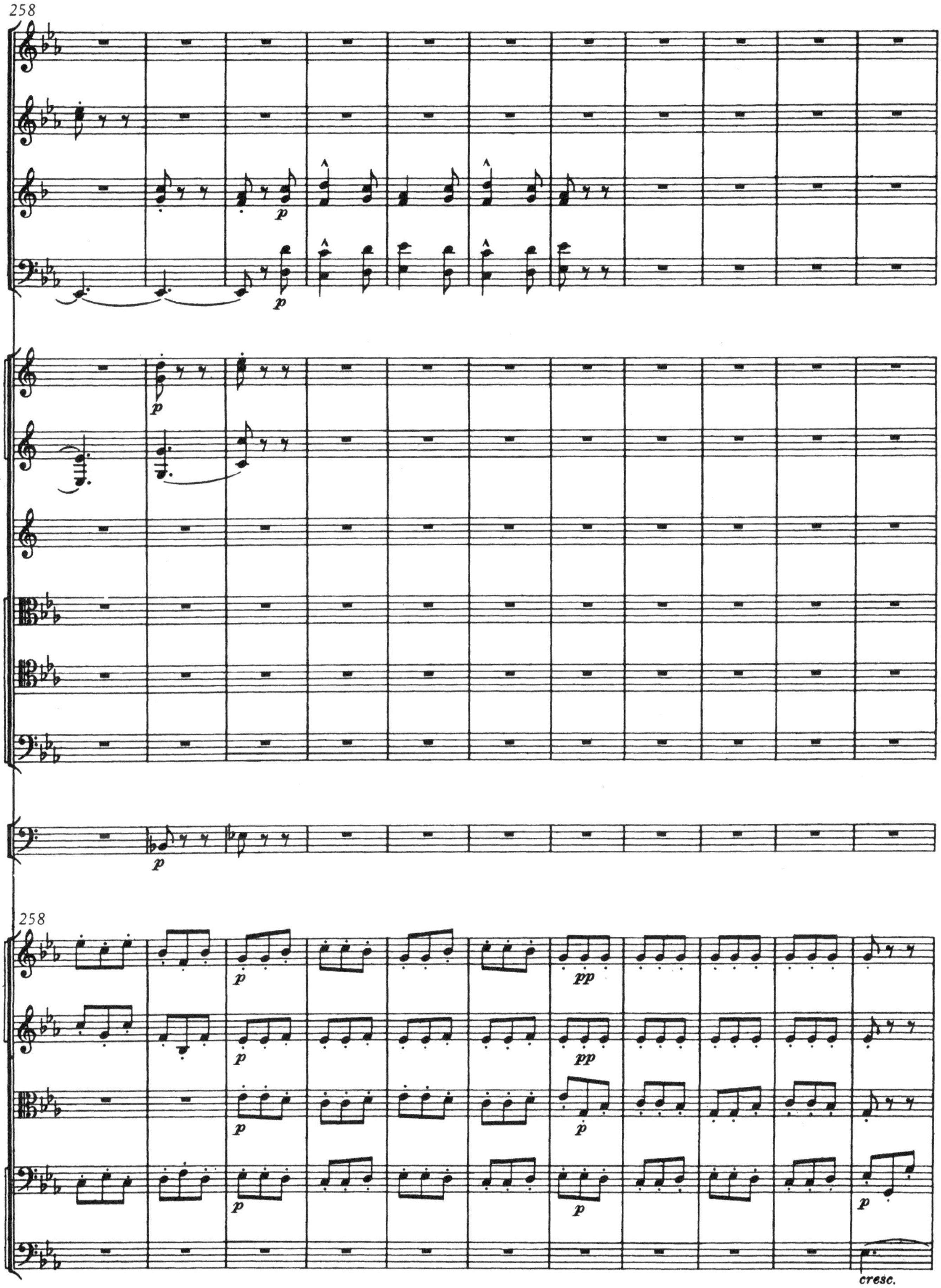
258
p
p
p
p
p
258
p
pp
p
pp
p
p
p
p
cresc.

269
rall.
ff
f cresc.
p
dim.
pp
muta in A
cresc.
p cresc.
in E
in E
in E
269
mf
f
rall.

TRIO

Allegro M. M. ♩ = 132

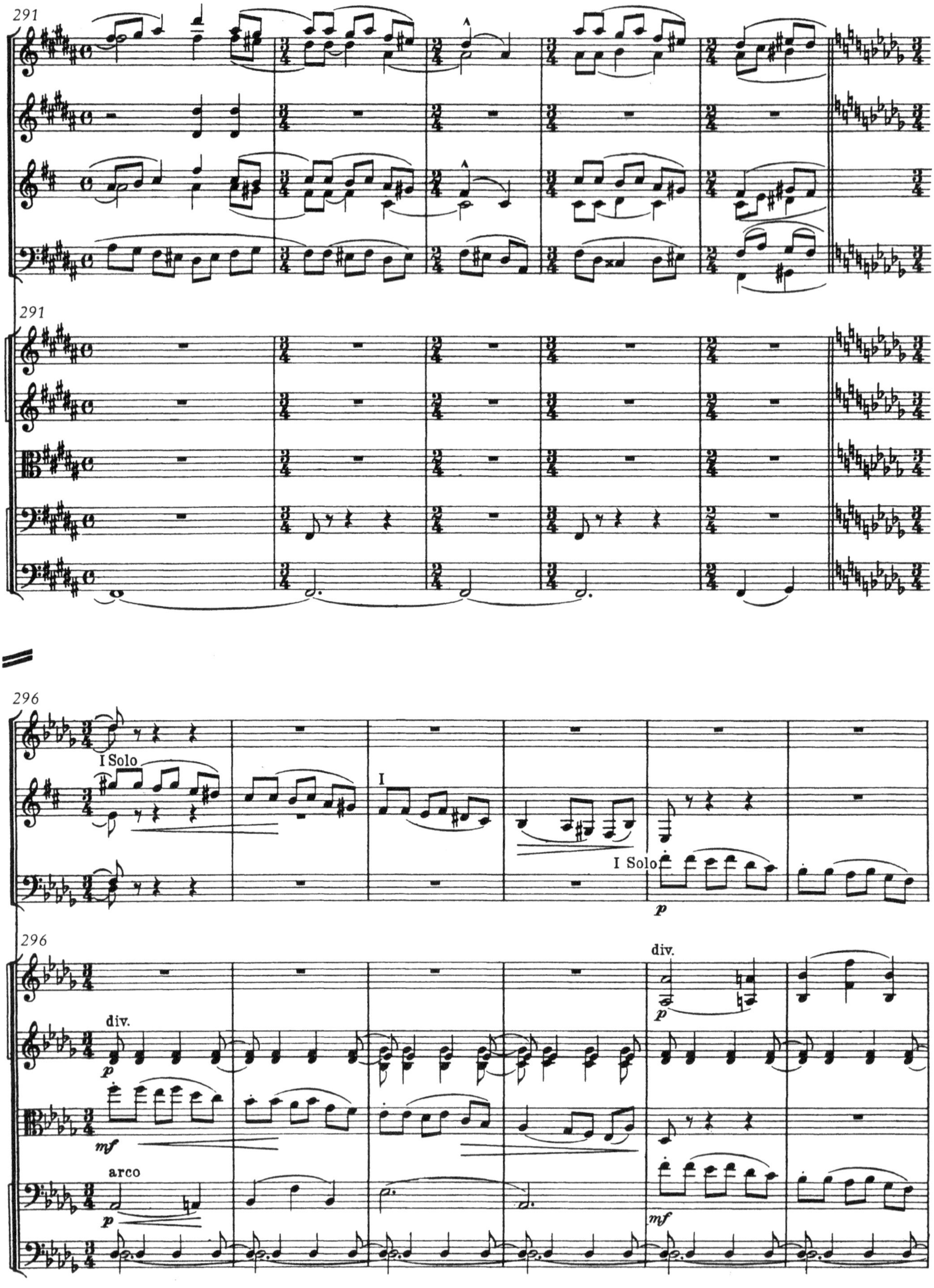
291
291
296
I Solo
I
I Solo
p
296
div.
div.
p
mf
arco
p
mf

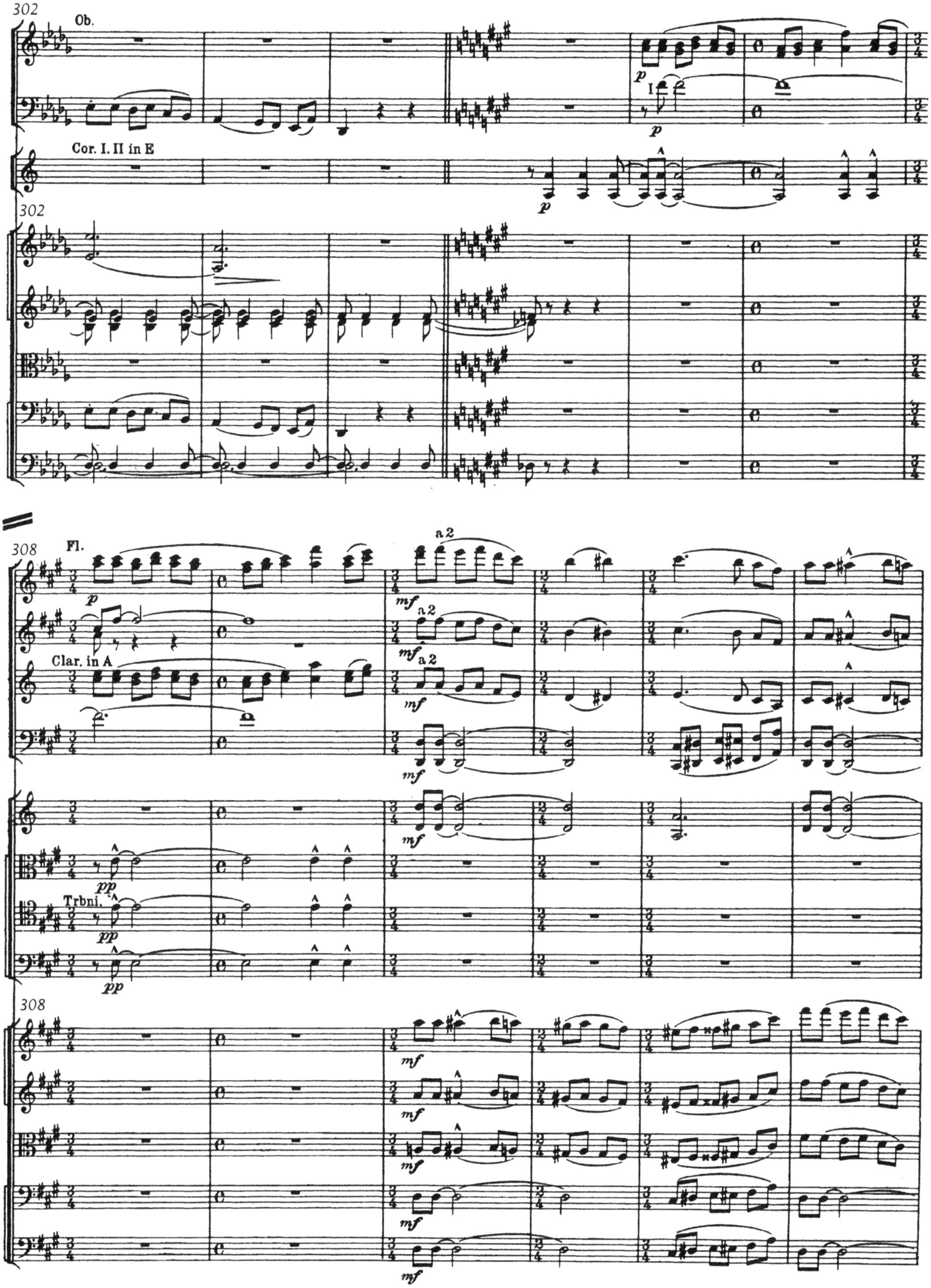
302
Ob.
I
Cor. I. II in E
302
308
Fl.
a 2
a 2
Clar. in A
a 2
Trbni.
308

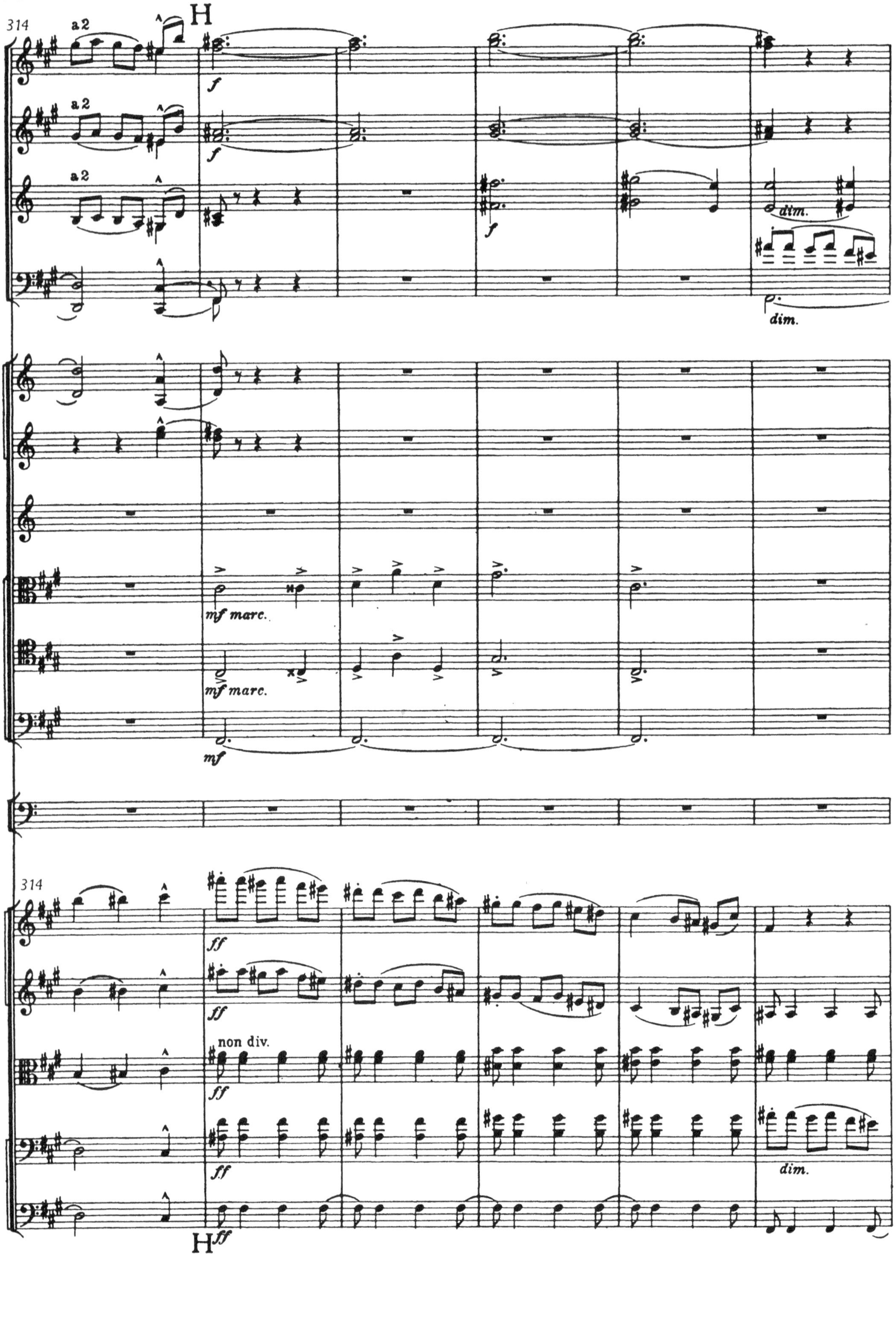
314
a2
H
f
dim.
mf marc.
mf
non div.
ff

320
Ob.
rall.
I a tempo
Cor. I. II in E
320
non div.
pizz.
pizz.
pizz.
rall.
I a tempo
326
326
pizz.

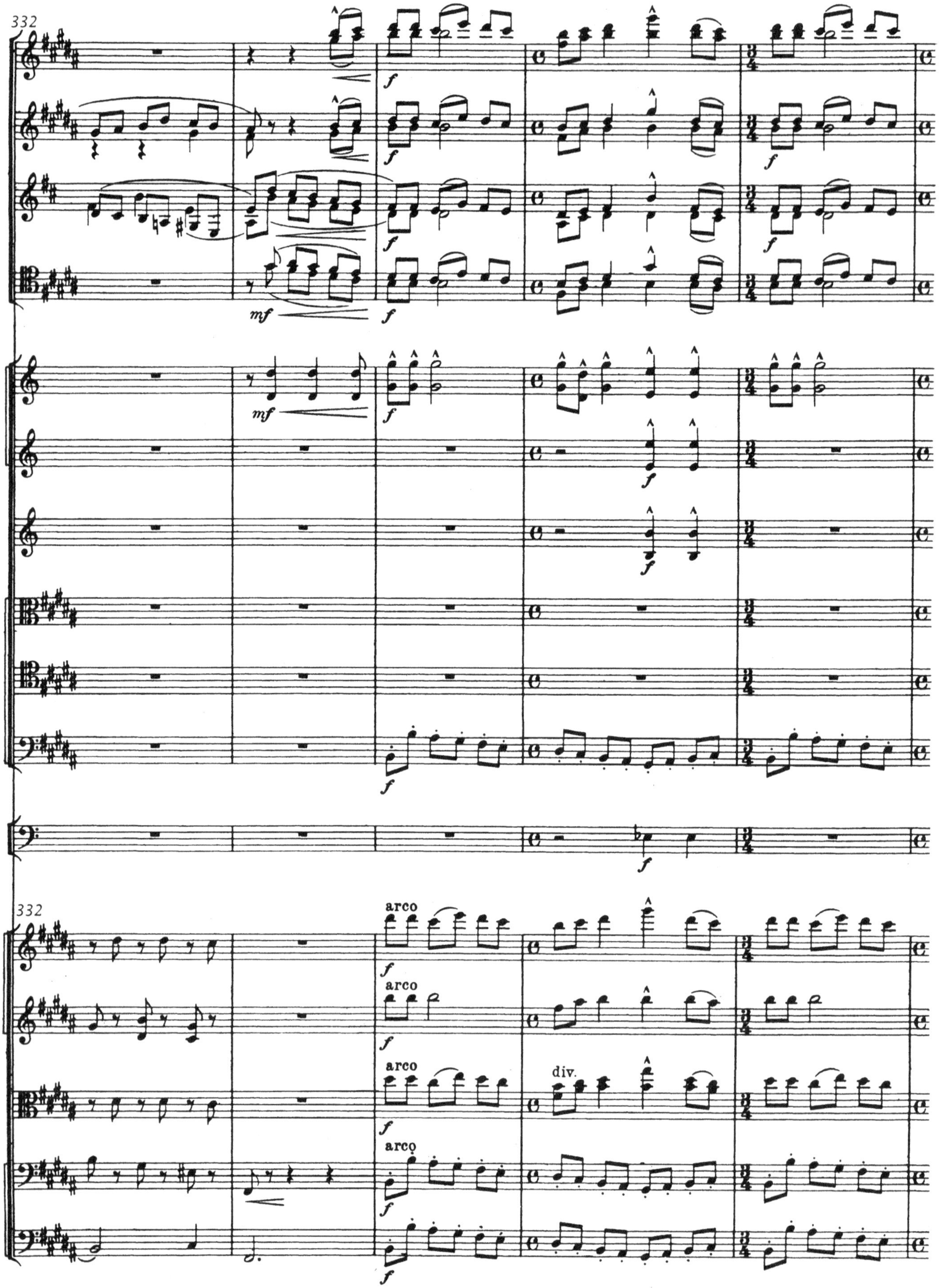
332
mf
f
332
arco
arco
arco
div.
arco

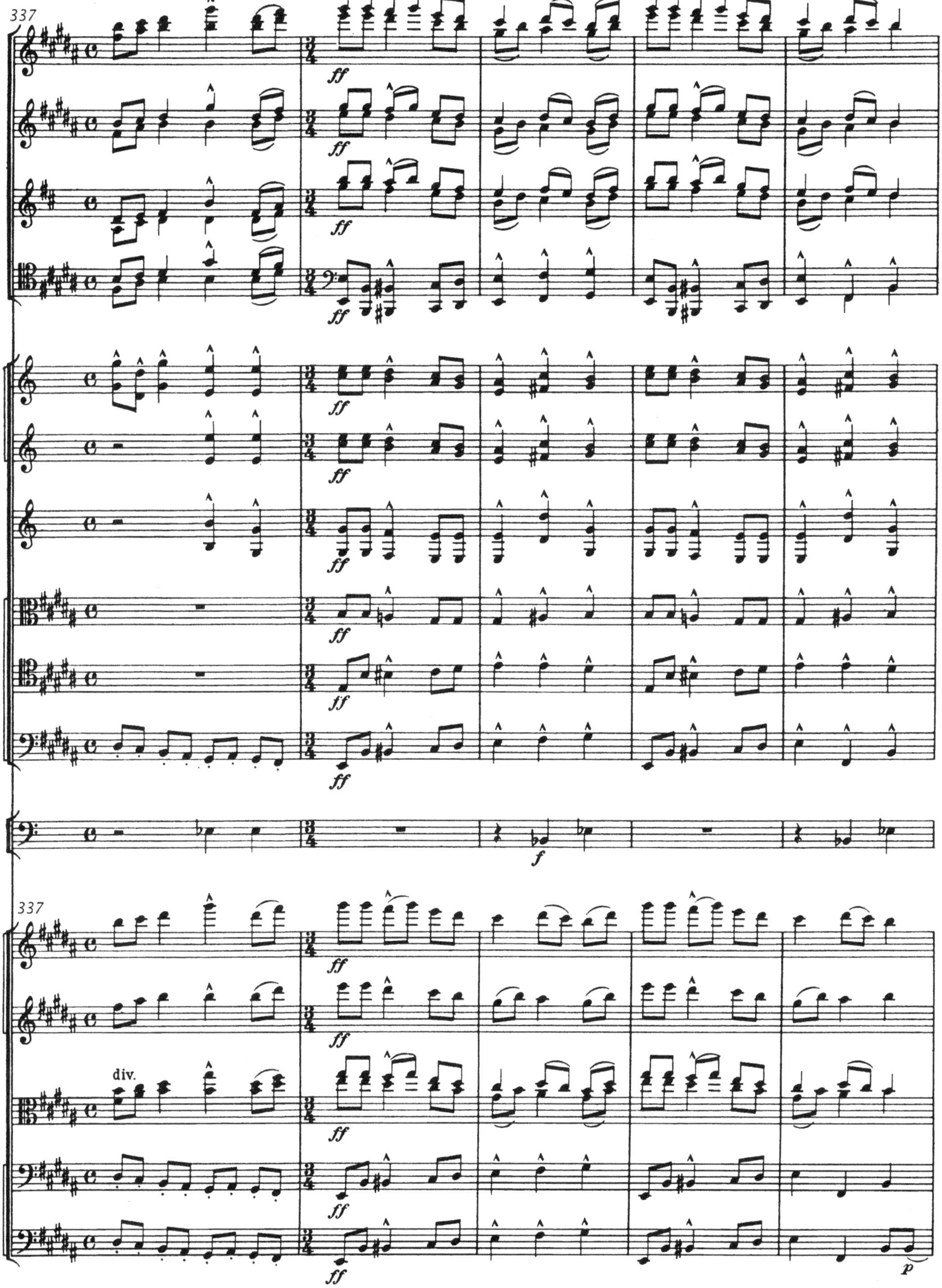
337
ff
f
div.
p

342
a 2
p
pp
dim.
342
dim.
348
rall.
a 2
in B
Cor. in E
in Es
in Es
348
rall.

354
Prestissimo
Ob.
Fag.
354
p
div.
legg.
pp
pizz.
p
arco
div.
legg.
pp
pizz.
p
div.
pp
pizz.
p
pizz.
p
Prestissimo
364
pp
cresc.
pp
pp
cresc.
pizz.
pp
cresc.

374
Fl.
A
p
p legg.
pp legg.
Clar. in B
pp legg.
p legg.
pp
Timp.
pp
374
pizz.
pizz.
pizz.
pp
pizz.
A
384
cresc.
I Solo
Cor. in Es
pp
384
non div.
non div.
cresc.

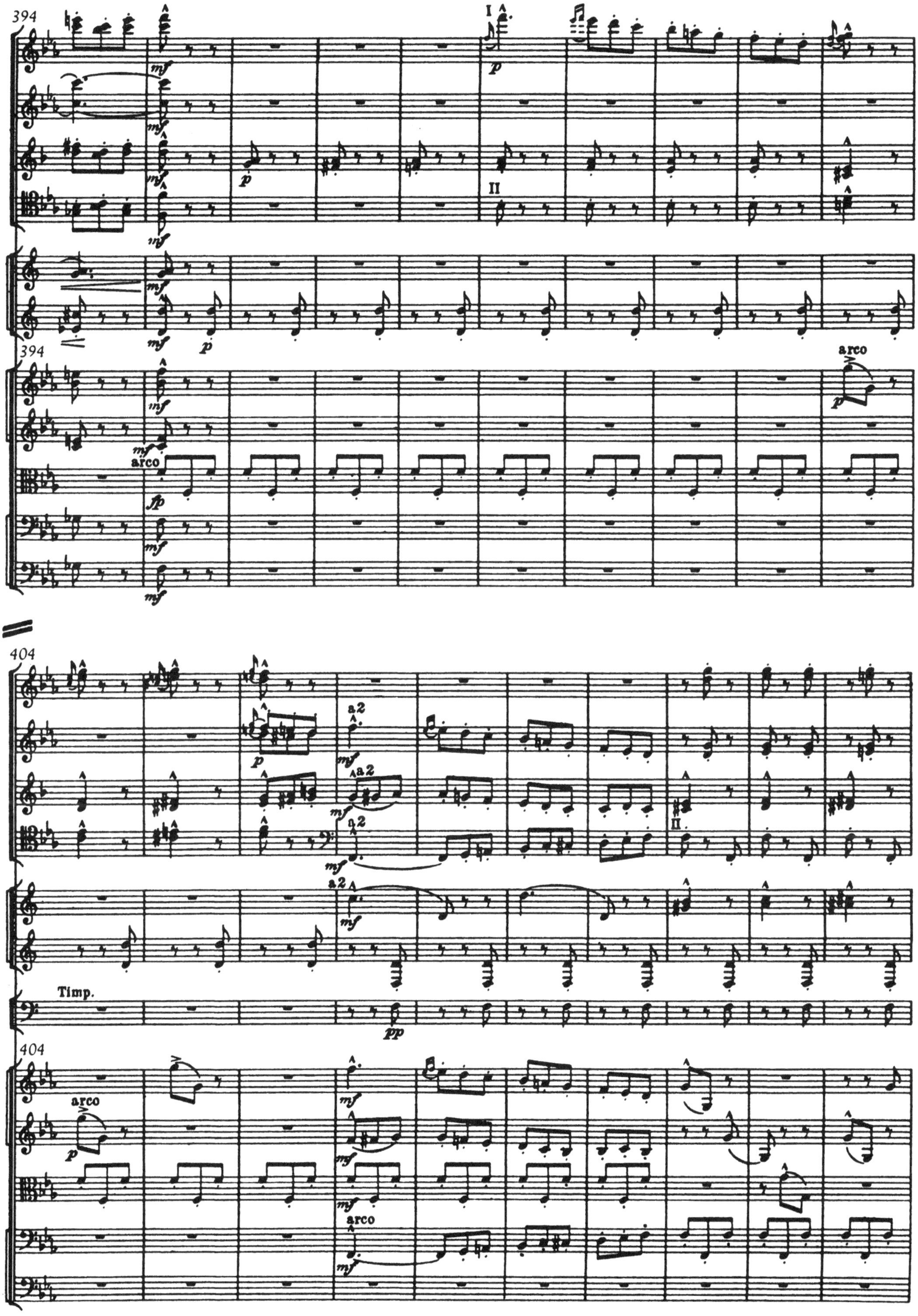
394
I
II
394
arco
arco
404
a 2
a 2
a 2
II
a 2
Timp.
404
arco
arco

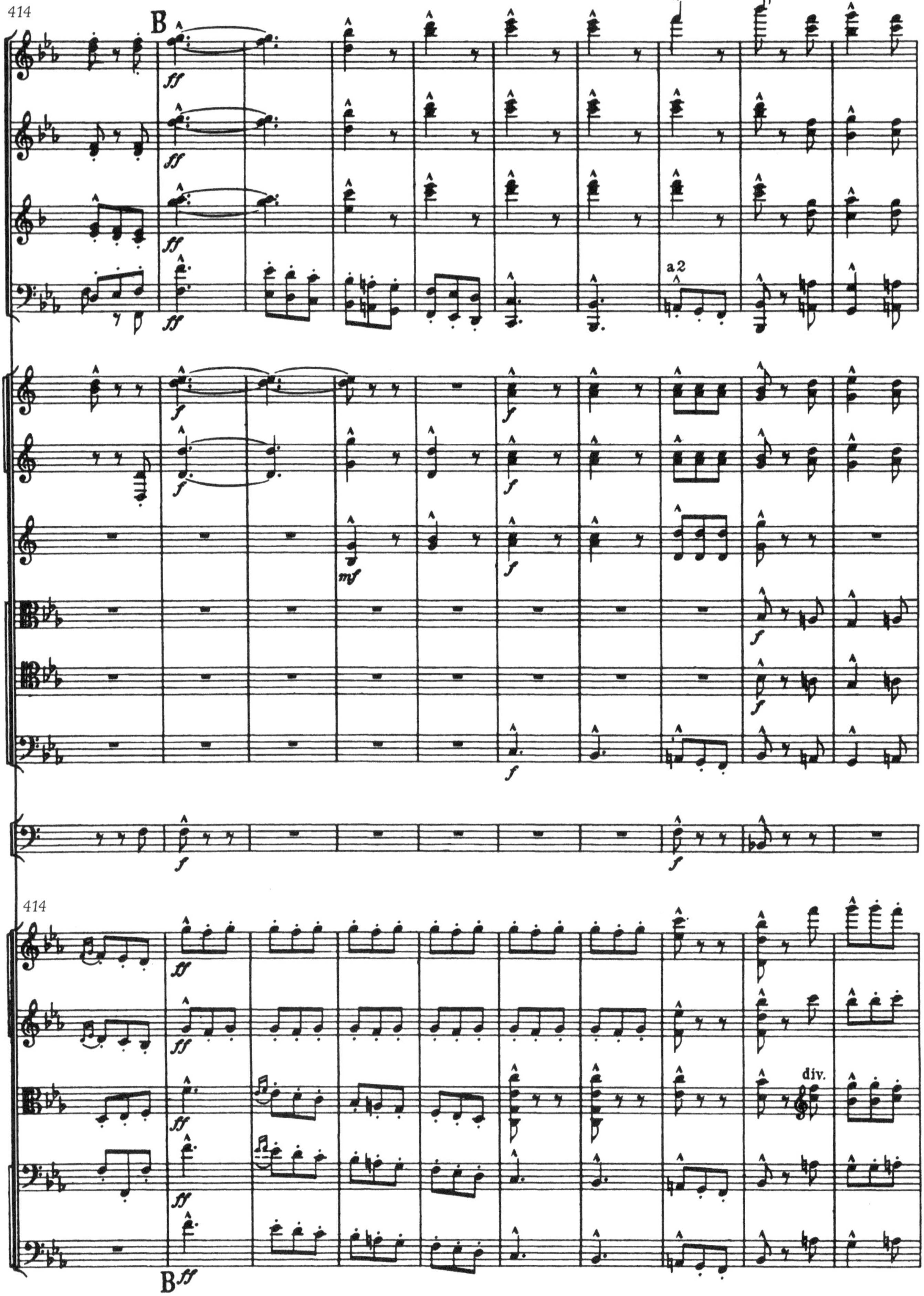
414
B
ff
a2
f
mf
414
div.
B ff

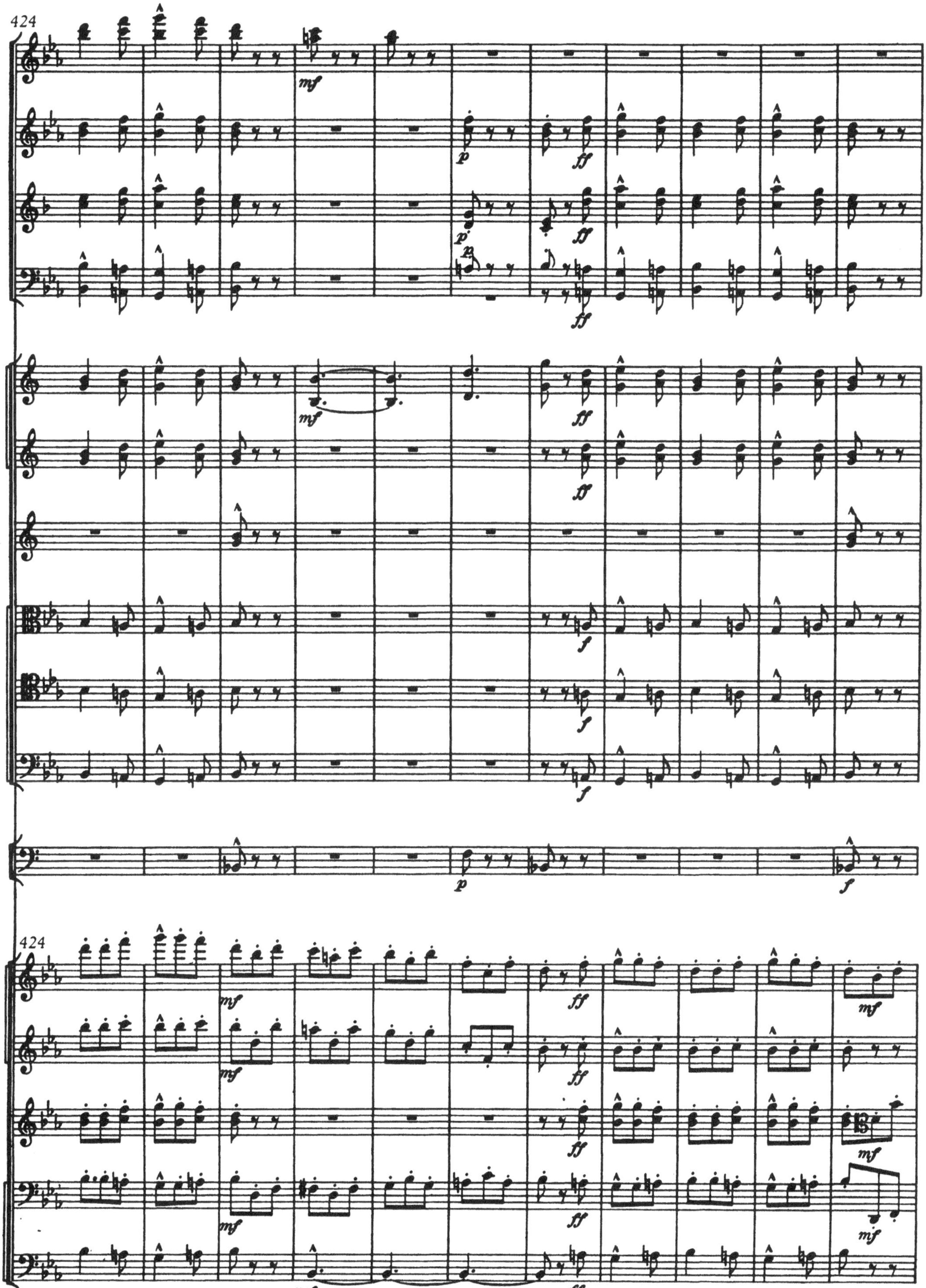

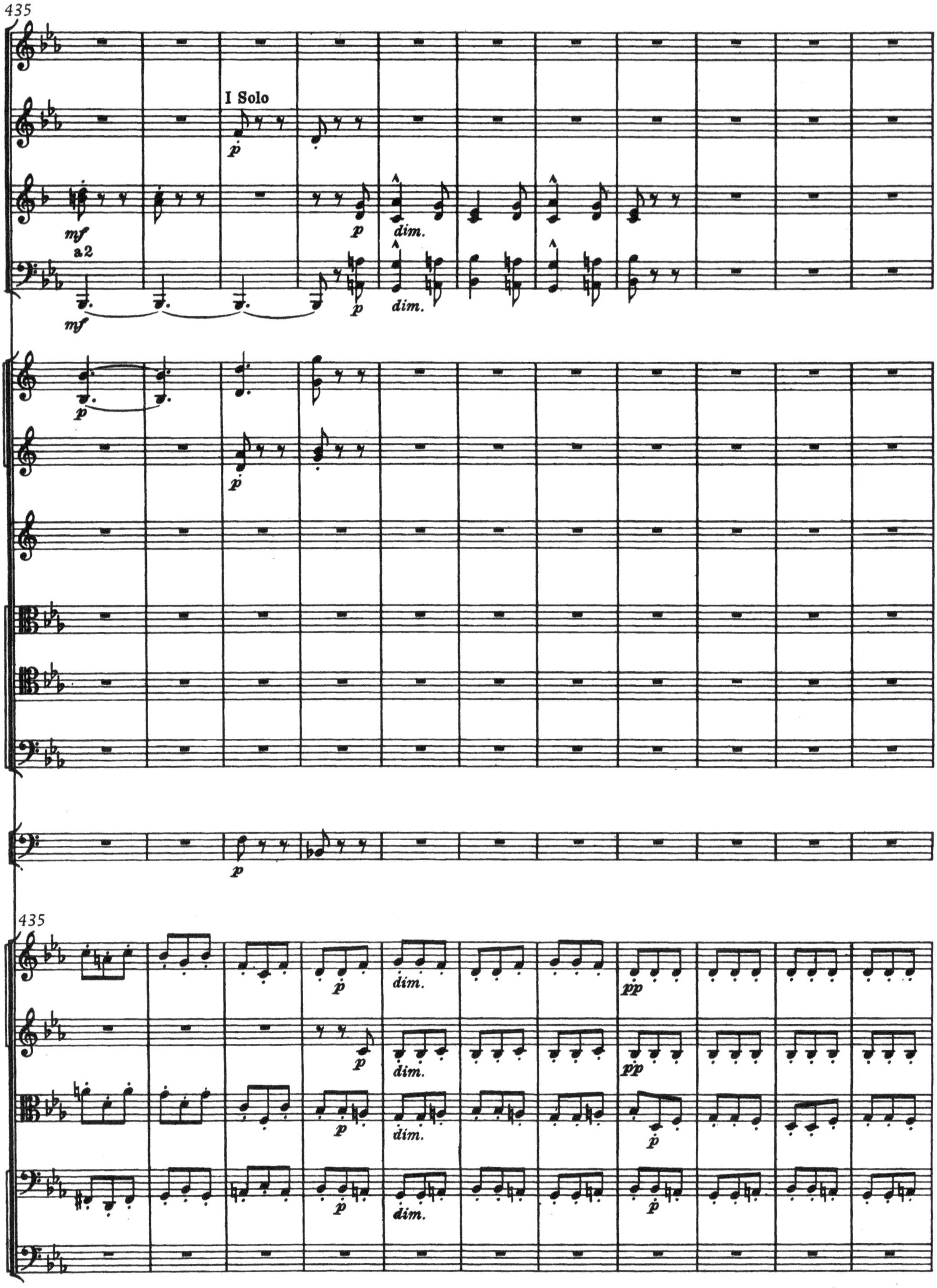
435
I Solo
a2
mf
p
dim.
pp
435

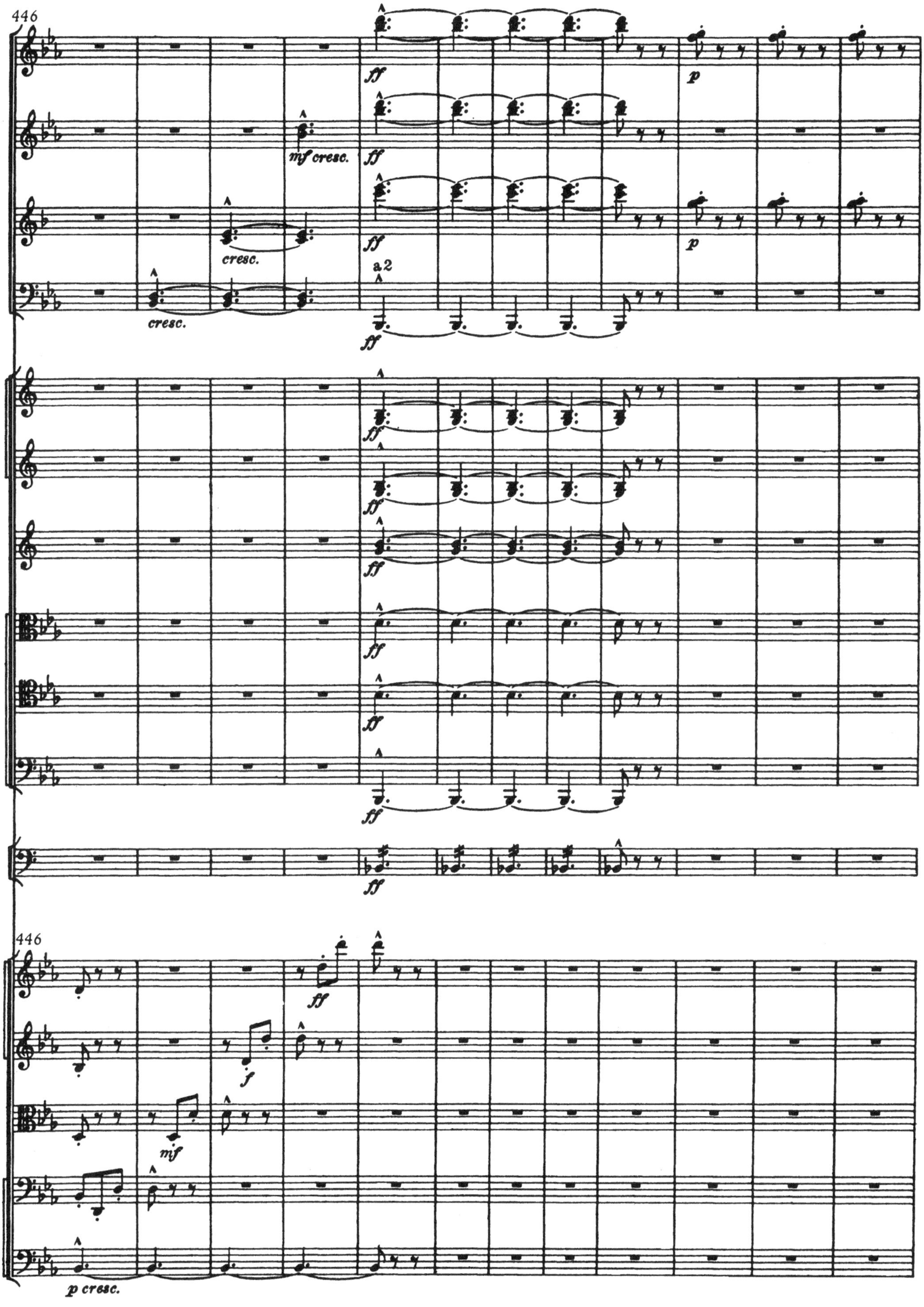
446
ff
p
mf cresc.
cresc.
a 2
f
mf
p cresc.

458
C
Fl.
Ob.
a 2
p marc.
Clar. in B
a 2
p cresc.
marc.
Cor. I. II in Es
a 2
p cresc.
marc.
458
p cresc.
cresc. poco a poco
p cresc.
pizz.
cresc. poco a poco
p
pizz.
p
C
469
f
f
f
a 2
f
f
mf
p
469
f
p
f
dim.
p
arco
f dim.
f
pizz.
p
arco
f dim.
p
pizz.
p

480
ff marc.
ff marc.
ff marc.
I fp
a 2
480
p
p
arco
div.
p
div.
p
489
a 2
a 2
a 2
ff
ff
dim.
dim.
ff
ff
Cor. III. IV in Es
Trbe in Es
mf
dim.
p
p
mf
mf
mf
489
ff marc.
ff marc.
dim.
dim.
f
f
dim.
dim.
f
f

92

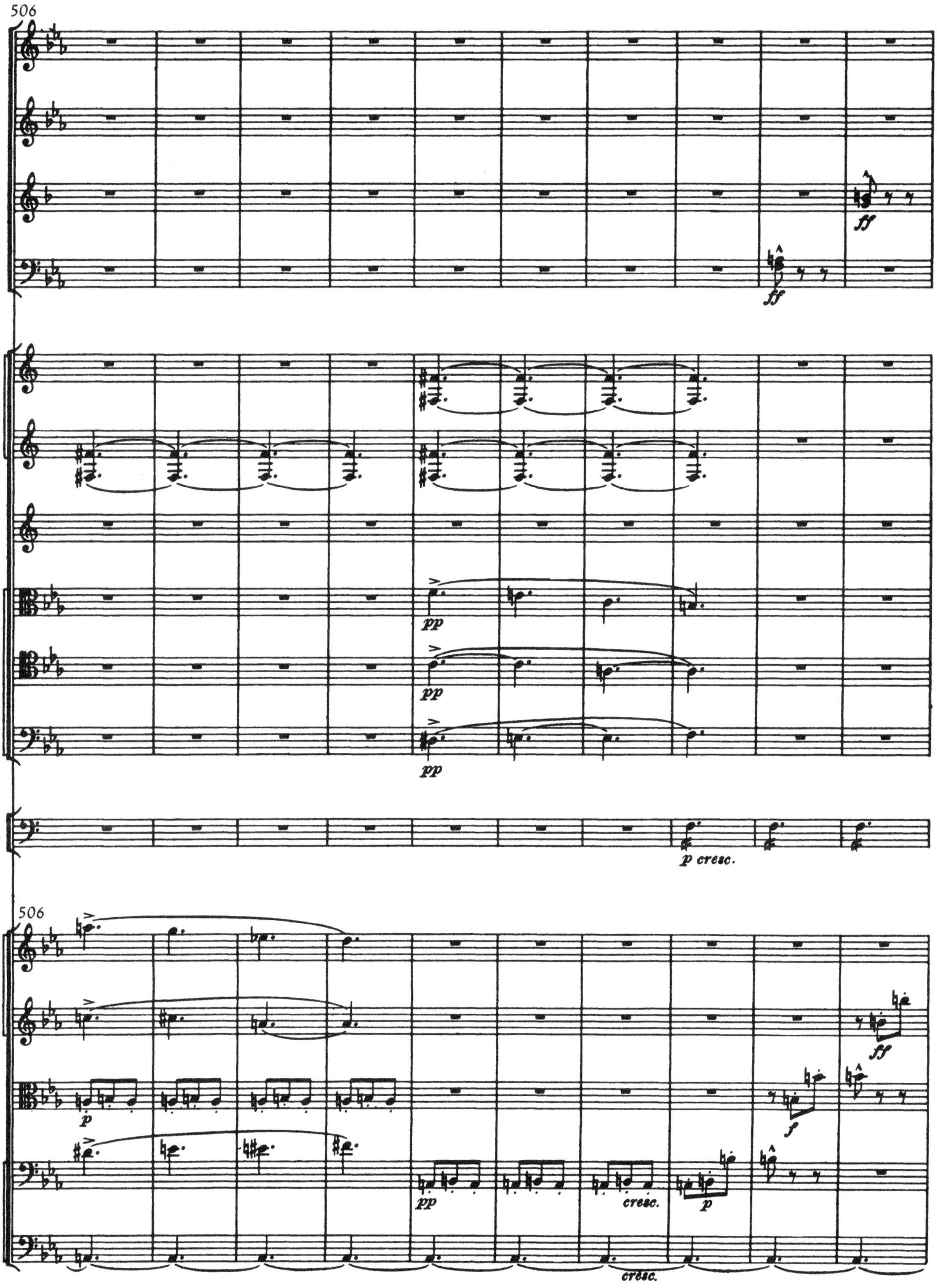
506
ff
ff
pp
pp
pp
p cresc.
506
ff
p
f
pp
cresc.
p
cresc.

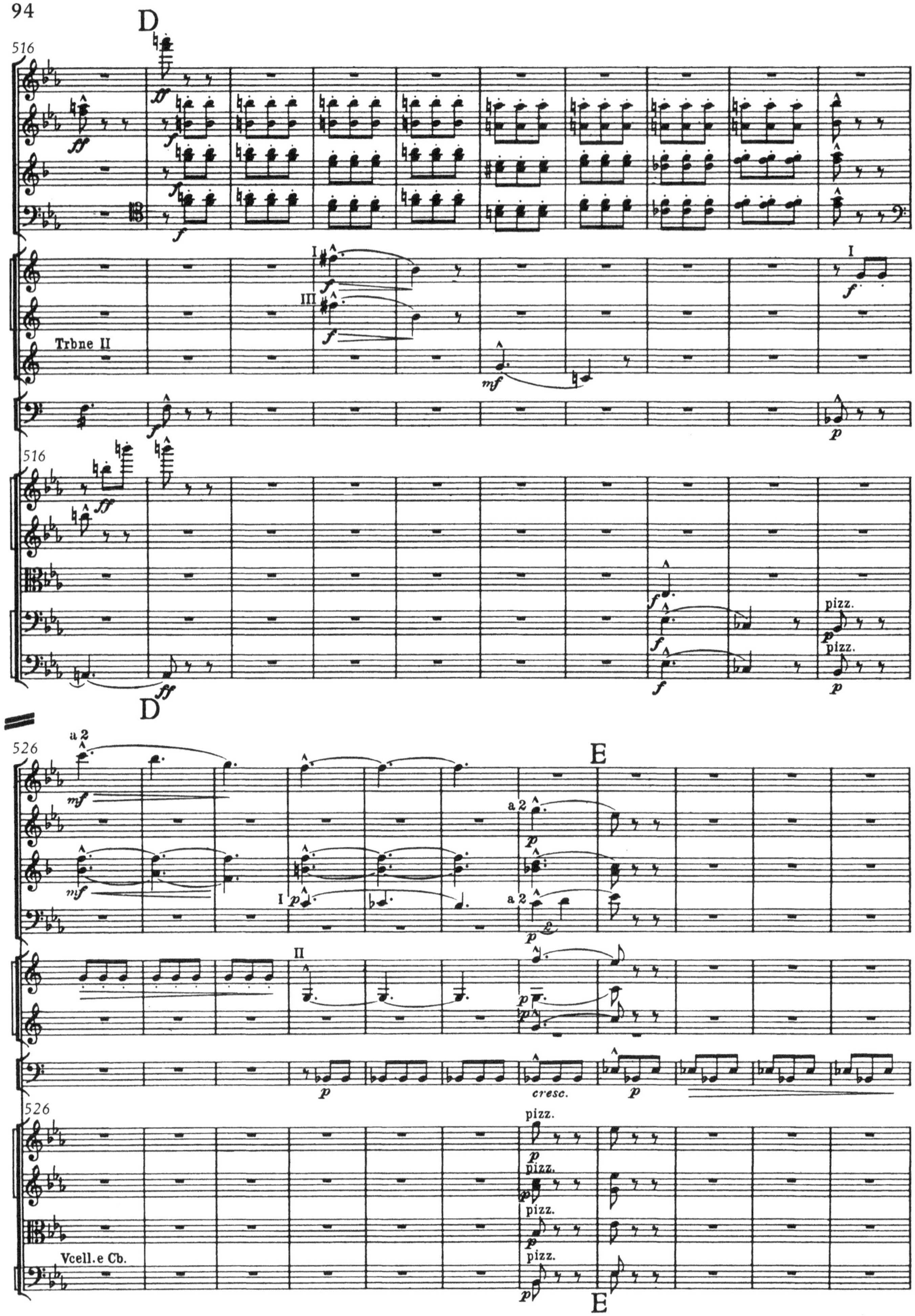
D
516
Trbne II
I
III
pizz.
D
a 2
526
E
a 2
I
II
cresc.
pizz.
Vcell. e Cb.
E

537
Fl.
p
I
pp
I
pp
pp
537
arco
div.
p
arco
div.
p
div.
arco
p
p
p
p
Vcell.
Cb.
547
547
p
p
p
pizz.
p
cresc.

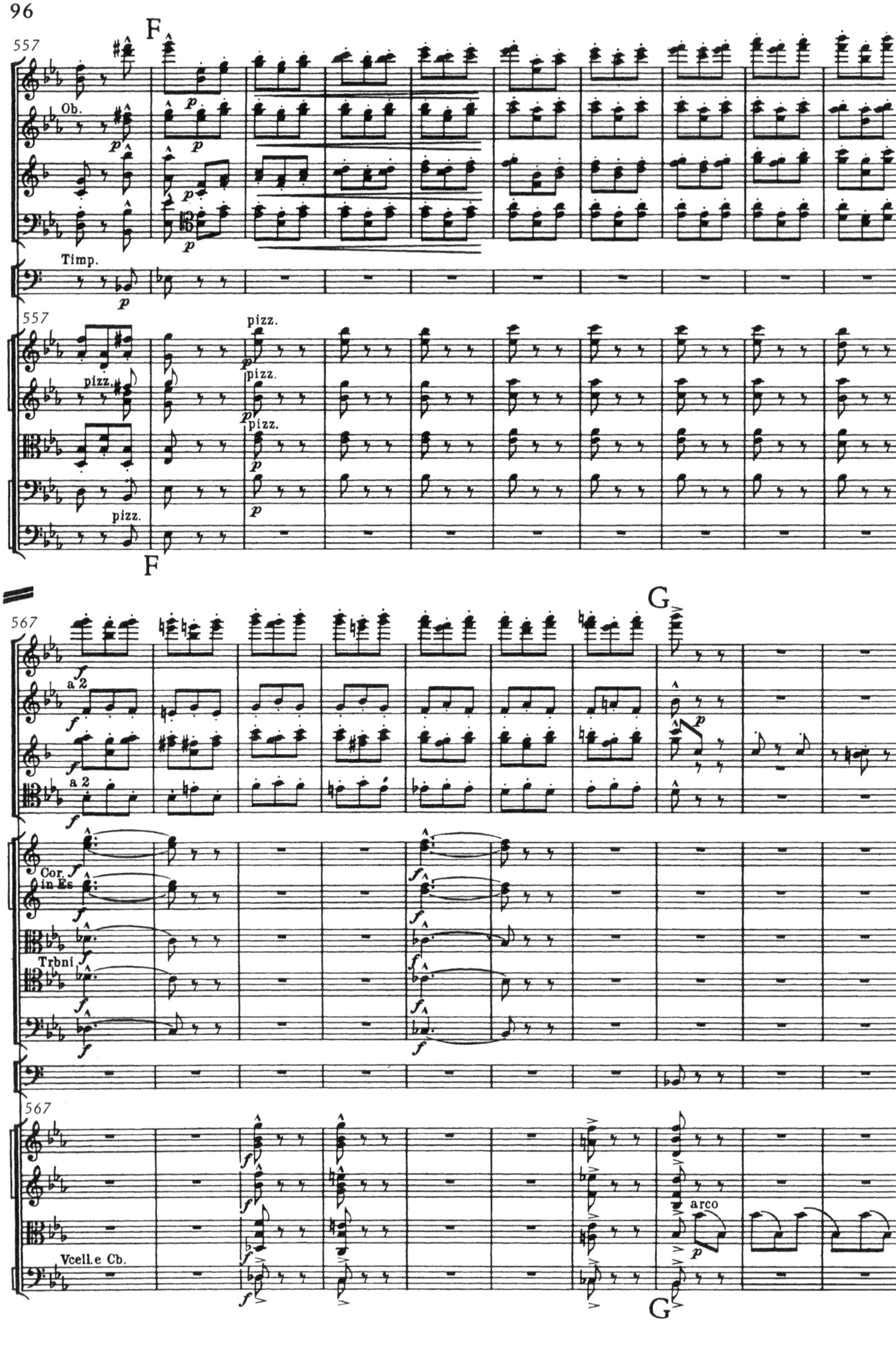
557
F
Ob.
p
Timp.
pizz.
567
G
a 2
f
arco
Cor. in Es
Trbni
Vcell. e Cb.

577
Fl.
I
p
I
p
577
arco
p
arco
p
Vcell.
Cb.
586
a 2
mf
Ob. a 2
mf
a 2
mf
a 2
mf
ff
ff
ff
ff
p
Cor. in Es
p
ff
ff
Timp.
p
f
586
mf
ff
mf
ff
mf
ff
arco
mf
ff
arco
mf
ff

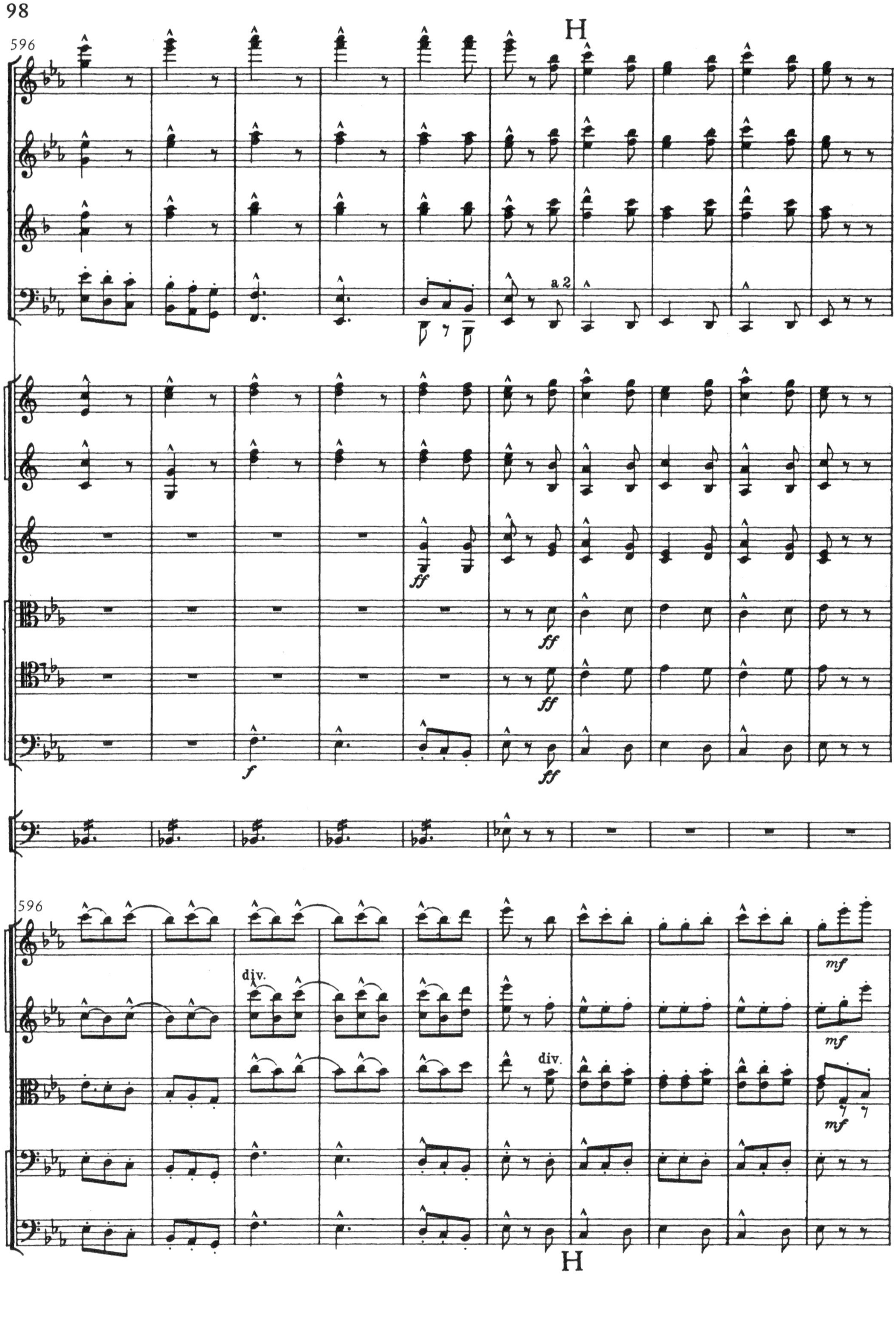
596
H
a 2
ff
f
596
div.
div.
mf
H

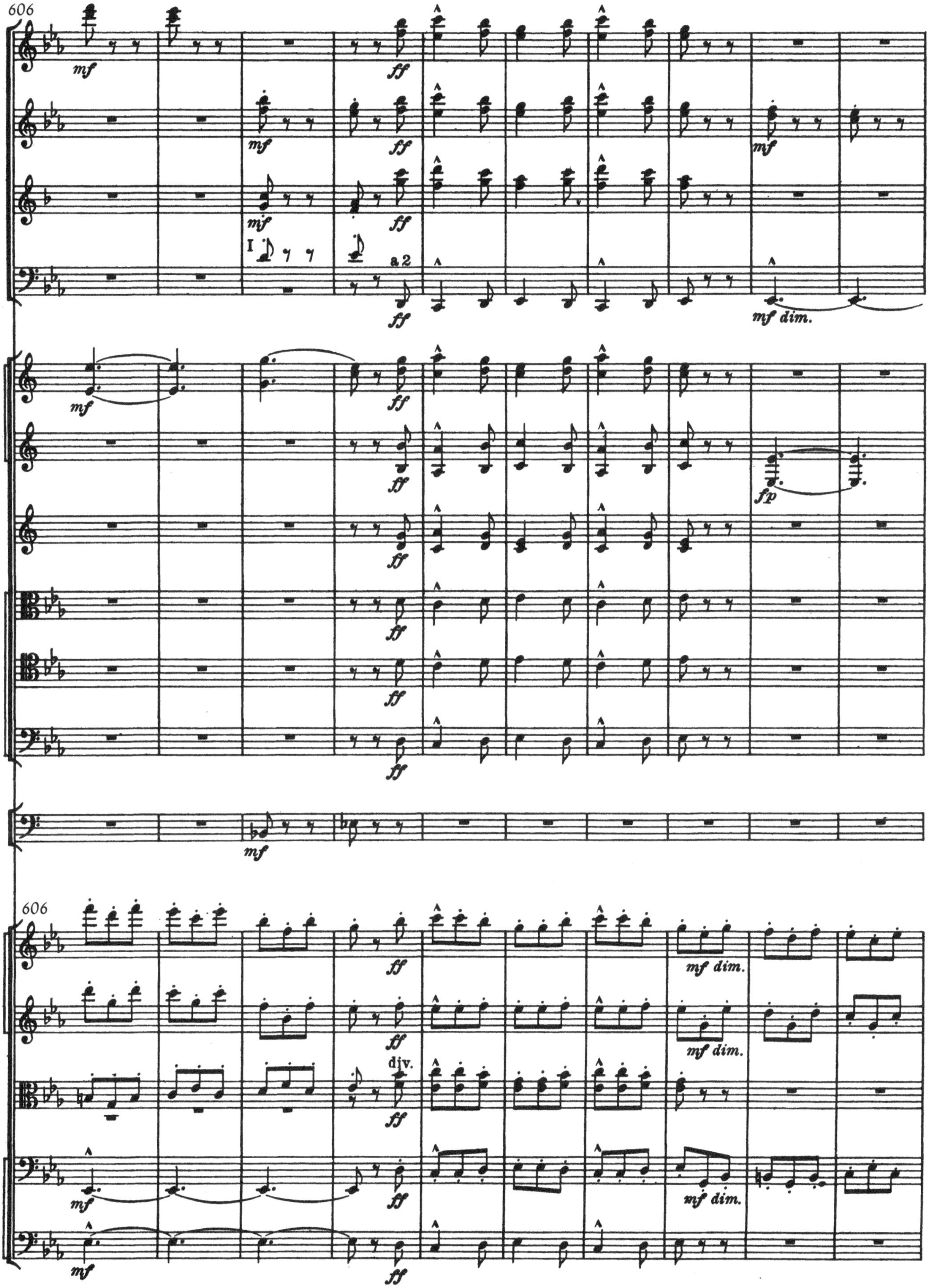
606
mf
ff
I
a 2
mf dim.
fp
div.
mf dim.

616
p
p
p
p
p
616
p
pp
p
pp
p
p
p
p
p
p
626
Ob.
I
p
p
p sempre cresc. e poco
p
a 2
p sempre cresc. e poco
p
p sempre cresc. e poco
Cor. I.II in Es
pp
p cresc. poco a poco
626
p sempre cresc. e poco
p cresc. poco a poco
p sempre cresc. e poco
p cresc. poco a poco
p sempre cresc. e poco
p sempre cresc. e poco
p cresc. poco a poco
p sempre cresc. e poco
I

640
a 2
mf
f
a 2
a poco più animato
mf
f
a 2
a poco più animato
mf
f
a poco più animato
mf
f
mf
640
a poco più animato
mf
f
a poco più animato
mf
f
a poco più animato
mf
f
a poco più animato
mf
f
a poco più animato
mf
f

652
K
ff
a 2
f marc. sempre
ff marc. sempre
f
p cresc.
marc. sempre
K marc. sempre

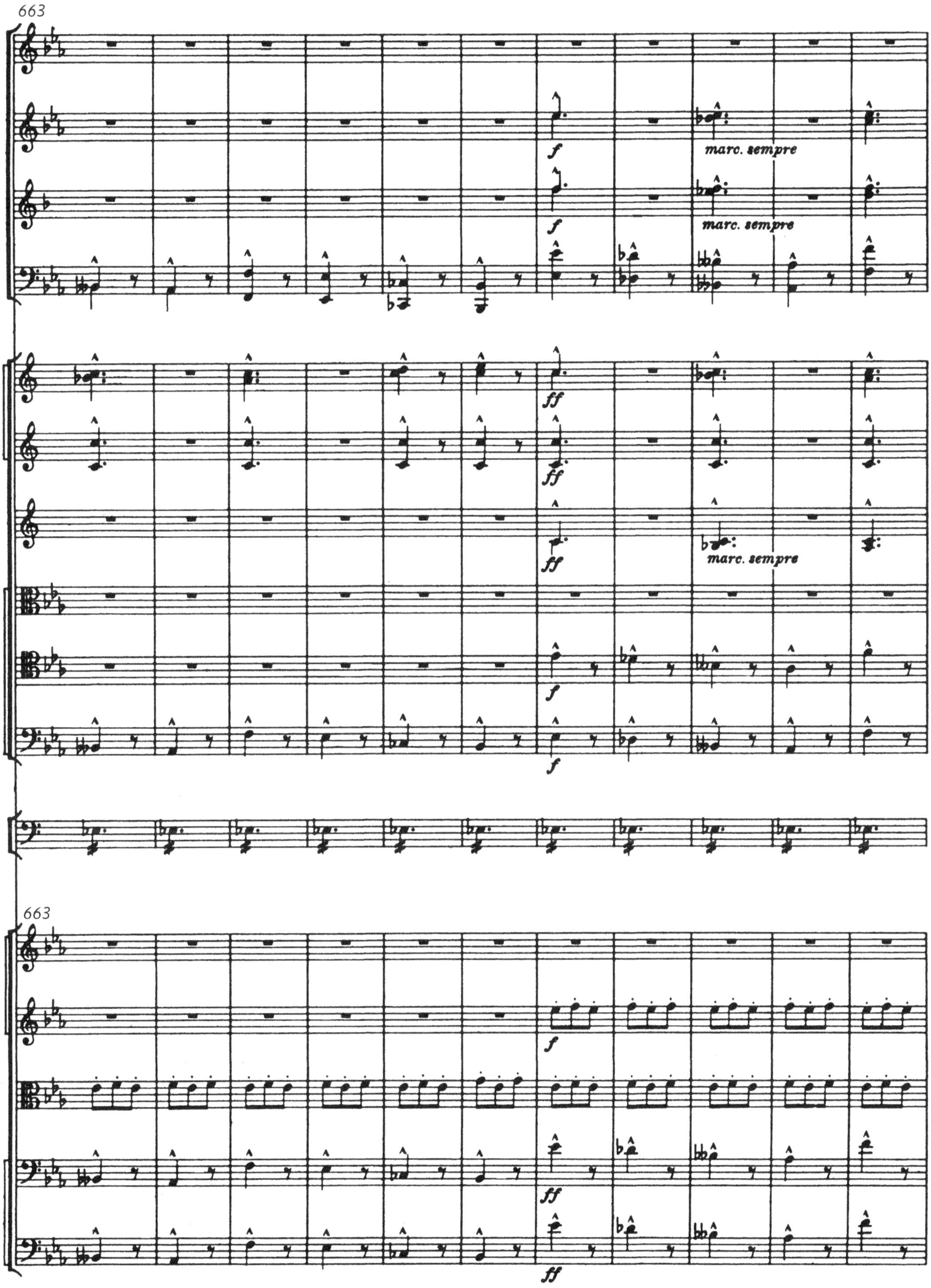
663
marc. sempre
marc. sempre
marc. sempre
663

674
ff marcato sempre
ff
ff
ff
ff
ff
ff
ff marcato sempre
ff
674
ff
ff
ff

685
a 2
a 2
a 2
a 2
a 2
ff
ff
ff
ff
ff
685
pizz.
arco
pizz.
arco
div.
pizz.
arco

III

9
marc.
marc.
9
15
15
p cresc.
p cresc.
p cresc.
cresc.
sf
sf
sf
sf marc.
div.
p cresc.

A
Fl.
Cor. ingl.
Fag. I
p
pp dolce ed espressivo
pp
dolce ed espressivo
sf
div. con sord.
div. con sord.
pp
Cor. II in D
II
p dolce ed espressivo

Lento
a tempo
Fl. I. II
Ob.
Clar. in A
Fag. I. II
a 2
Solo ad lib.
espressivo e cant.
Cor. in D
pesante marc.
Cor. III. IV in D
cresc.
senza sord.
p cantabile ed espressivo
cantabile ed espressivo

39
B
Fl.
fp dim.
pp
Ob.
Cor. ingl.
p dolce cantabile ed espressivo
Cor. I.II in D
cresc.
Timp.
39
div.
pizz.
div.
pizz.
B

44
Cor. III. IV in D
pp
44
arco
con sord.
pp
arco
con sord.
p
ppp
pizz.
pp
50
Fl.
Ob.
Clar. in A
pp
dim.
50
div.
arco
pp dolce

55
pp
pp
p dolce
I
pp
ppp
55
p
61
p
p
p marc.
pp marc
p
p
marc.
Fag. I
pp marc.
p
pp
61

66
C
cresc.
mf cresc.
f
p cresc. marc.
p cresc.
mf marc. cresc.
mf marc. cresc.
66
senza sord.
mf cresc.
cresc. marc.
arco
C

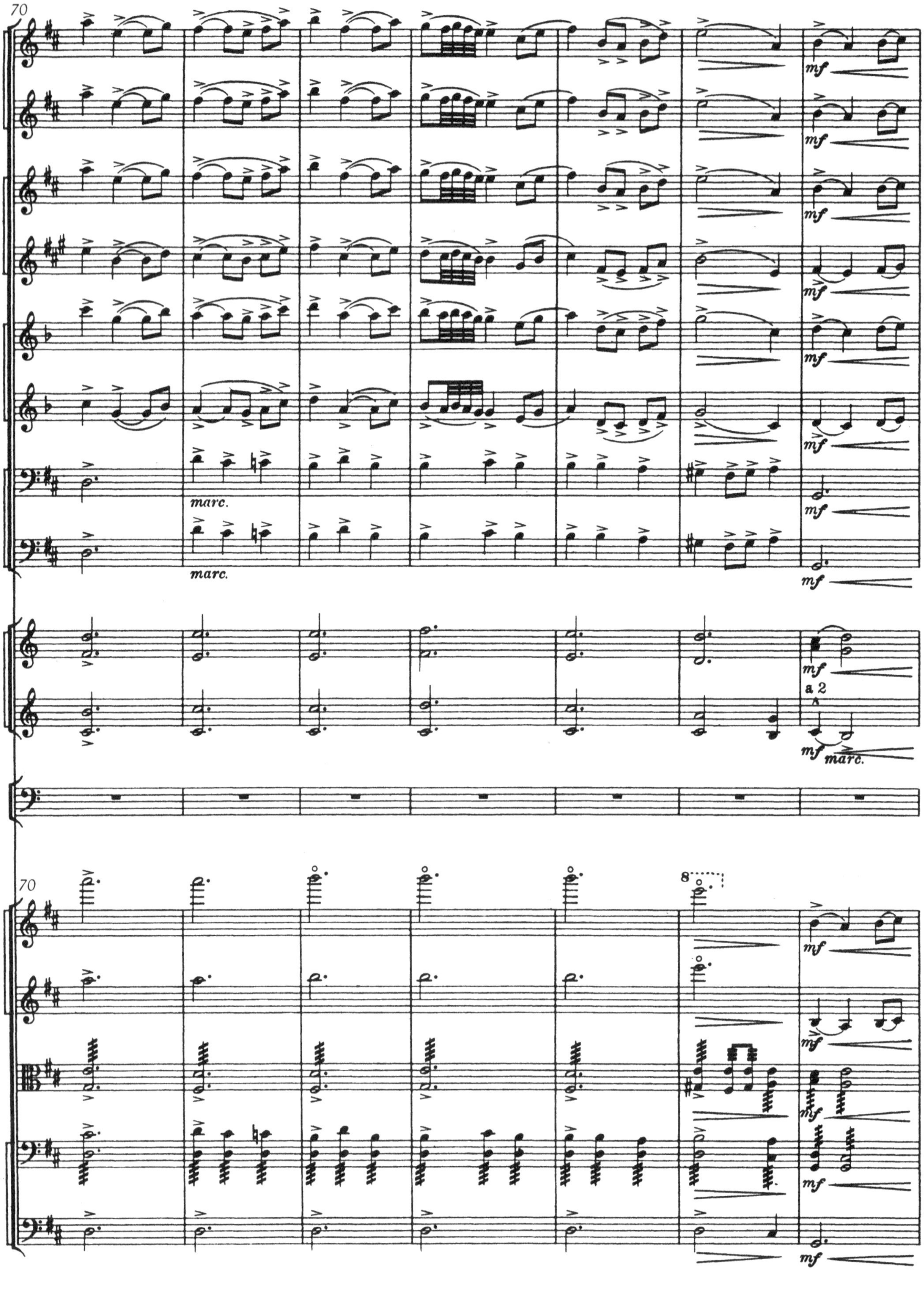
70
marc.
marc.
mf
a 2
mf marc.
70
8
mf

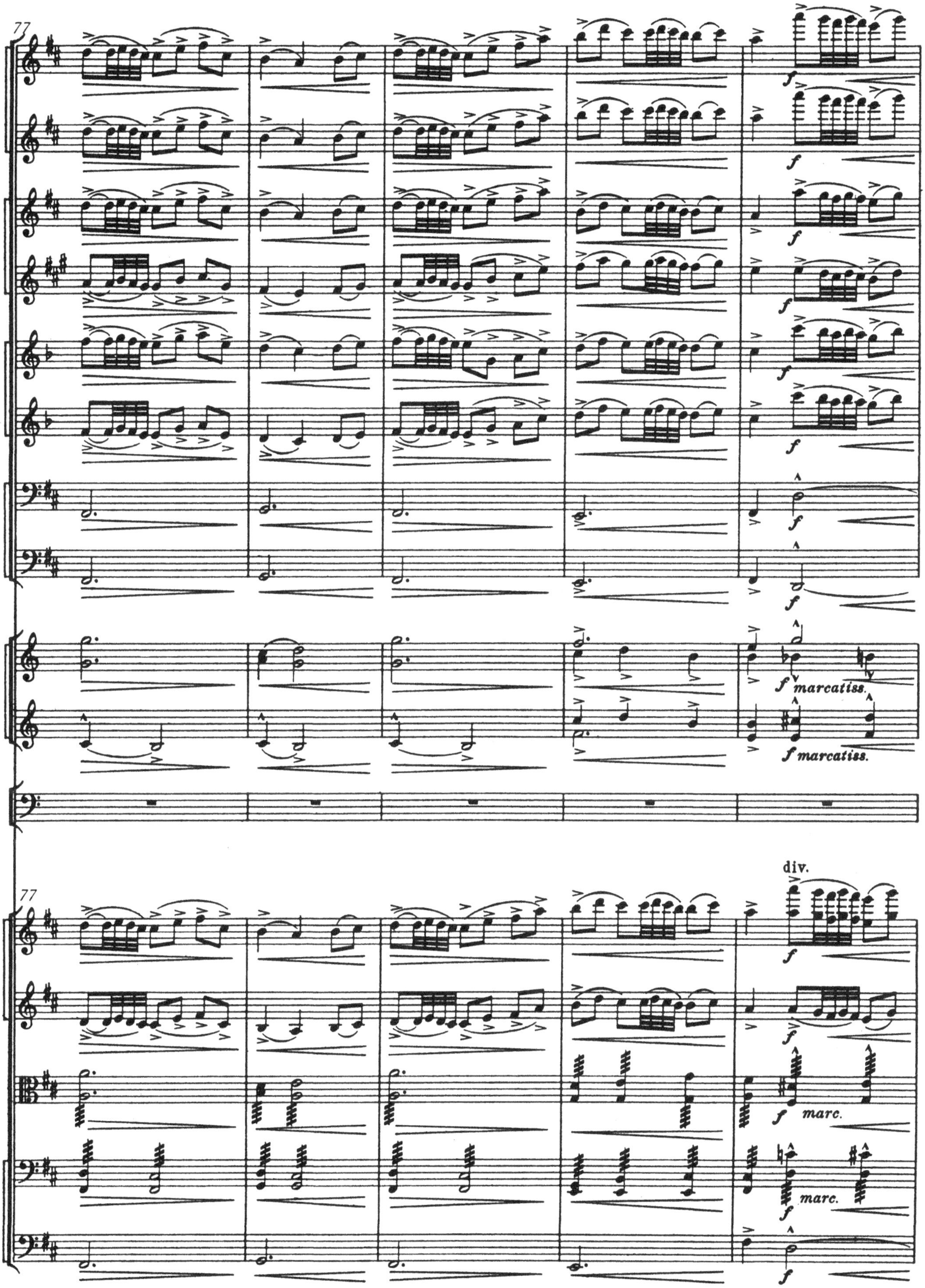
77
f
f marcatiss.
f marcatiss.
77
div.
f marc.
marc.

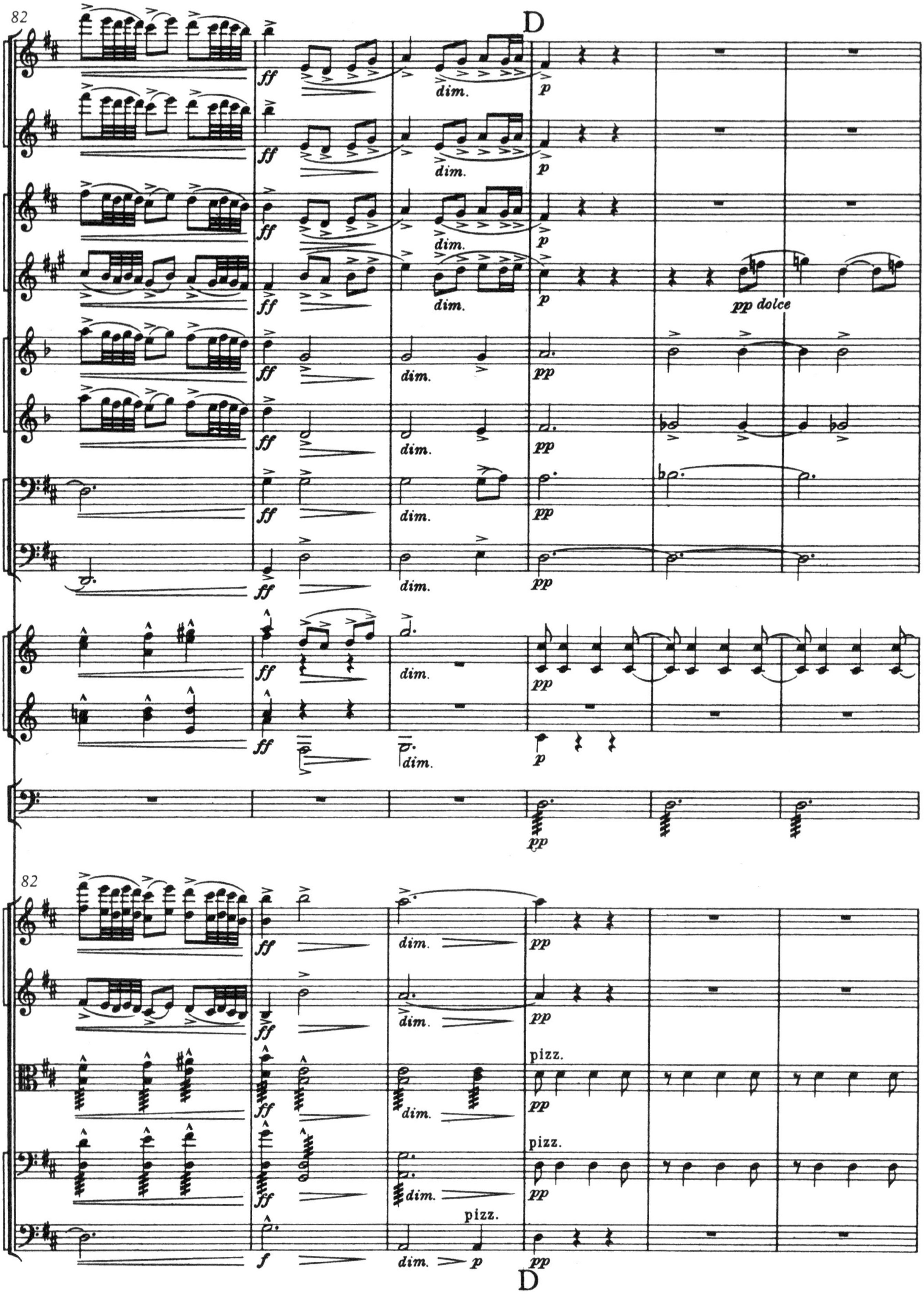
82
D
ff
dim.
p
pp dolce
pp
f
pizz.

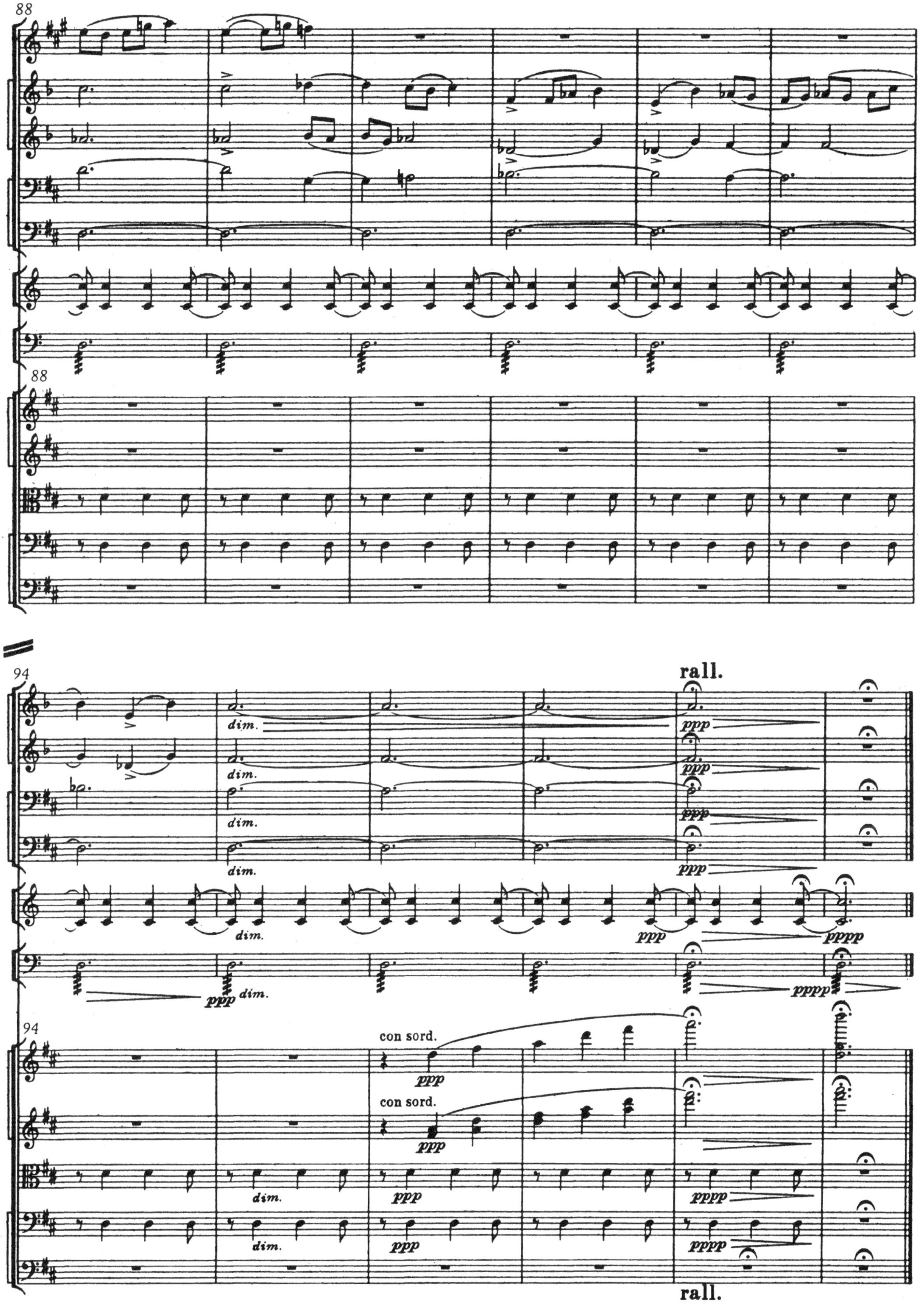
88
88
94
rall.
dim.
ppp
pppp
con sord.
94
rall.

IV

Allegro molto vivo M. M. ♩ = 168

2 Flauti

2 Oboi

2 Clarinetti in B

2 Fagotti

4 Corni in Es

2 Trombe in Es

3 Tromboni

Timpani

Violini I

Violini II

Viola

Violoncelli

Contrabassi

Allegro molto vivo M. M. ♩ = 168

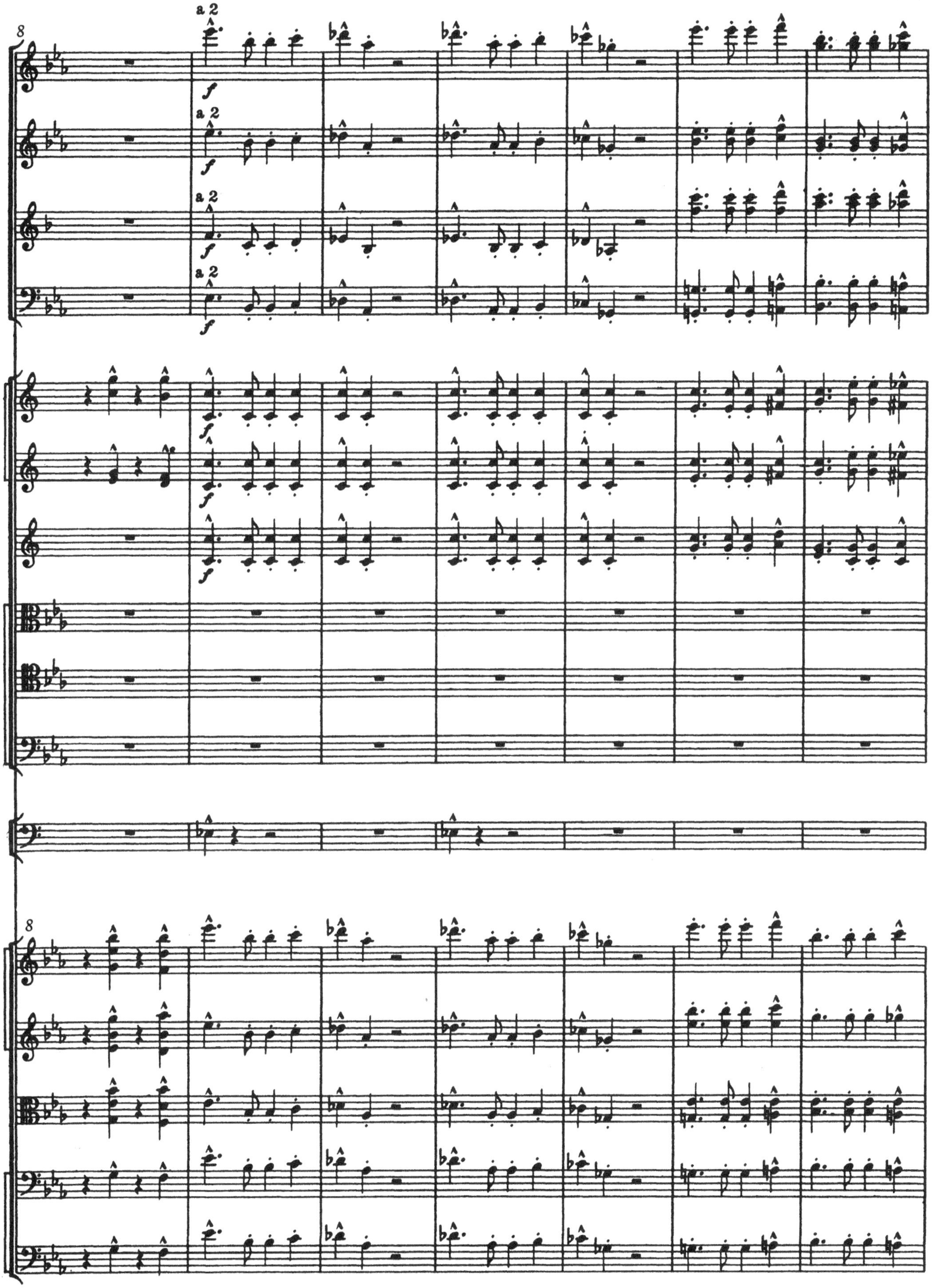
8
a 2
f
a 2
f
a 2
f
a 2
f
f
f
f
8

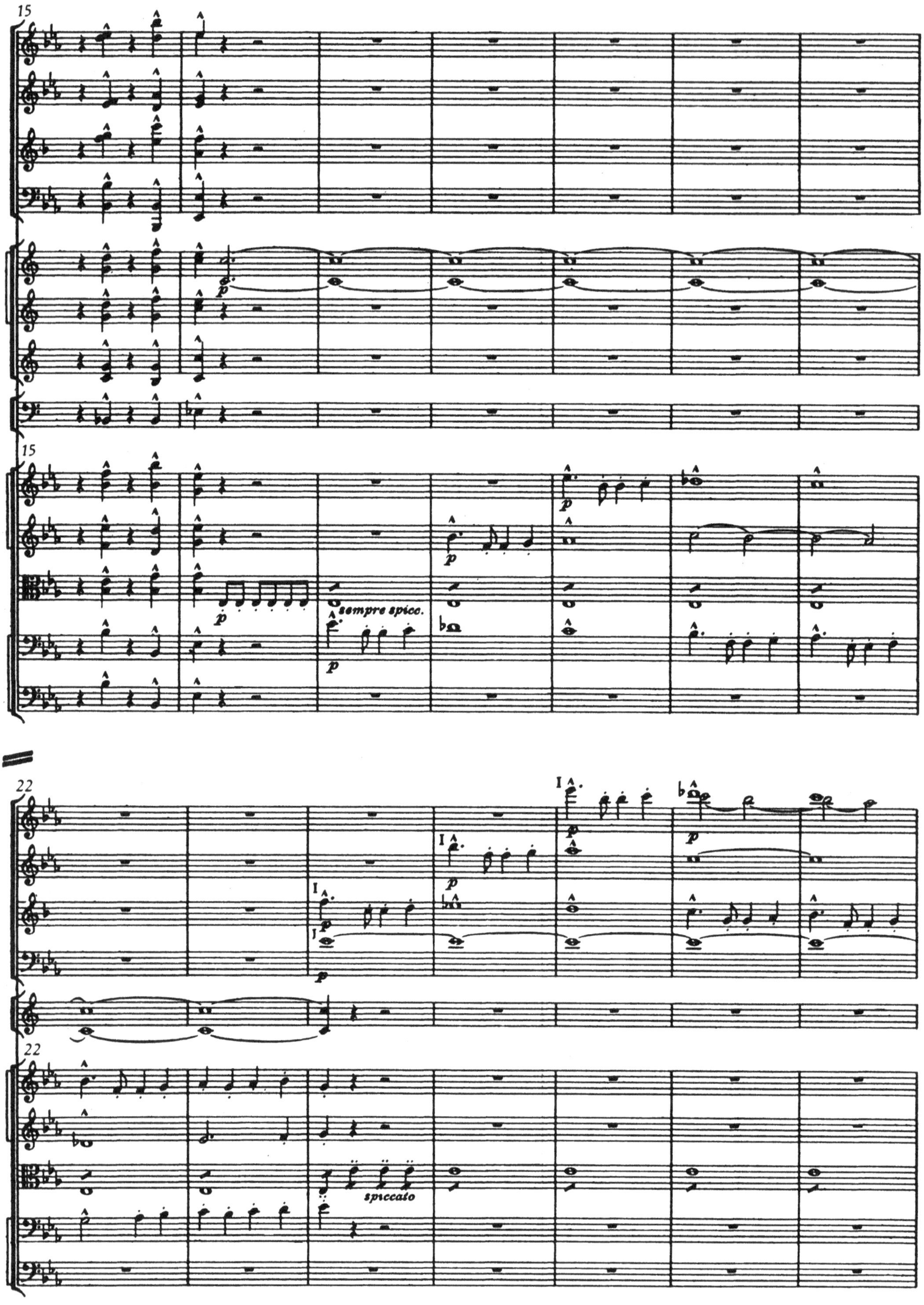
15
sempre spicc.
22
spiccato

29
a 2
I
cresc.
p cresc.
p
p cresc. poco a poco
36
A
a 2
Cor. in Es
Trbne III
f marc.
Timp.
div.
ff

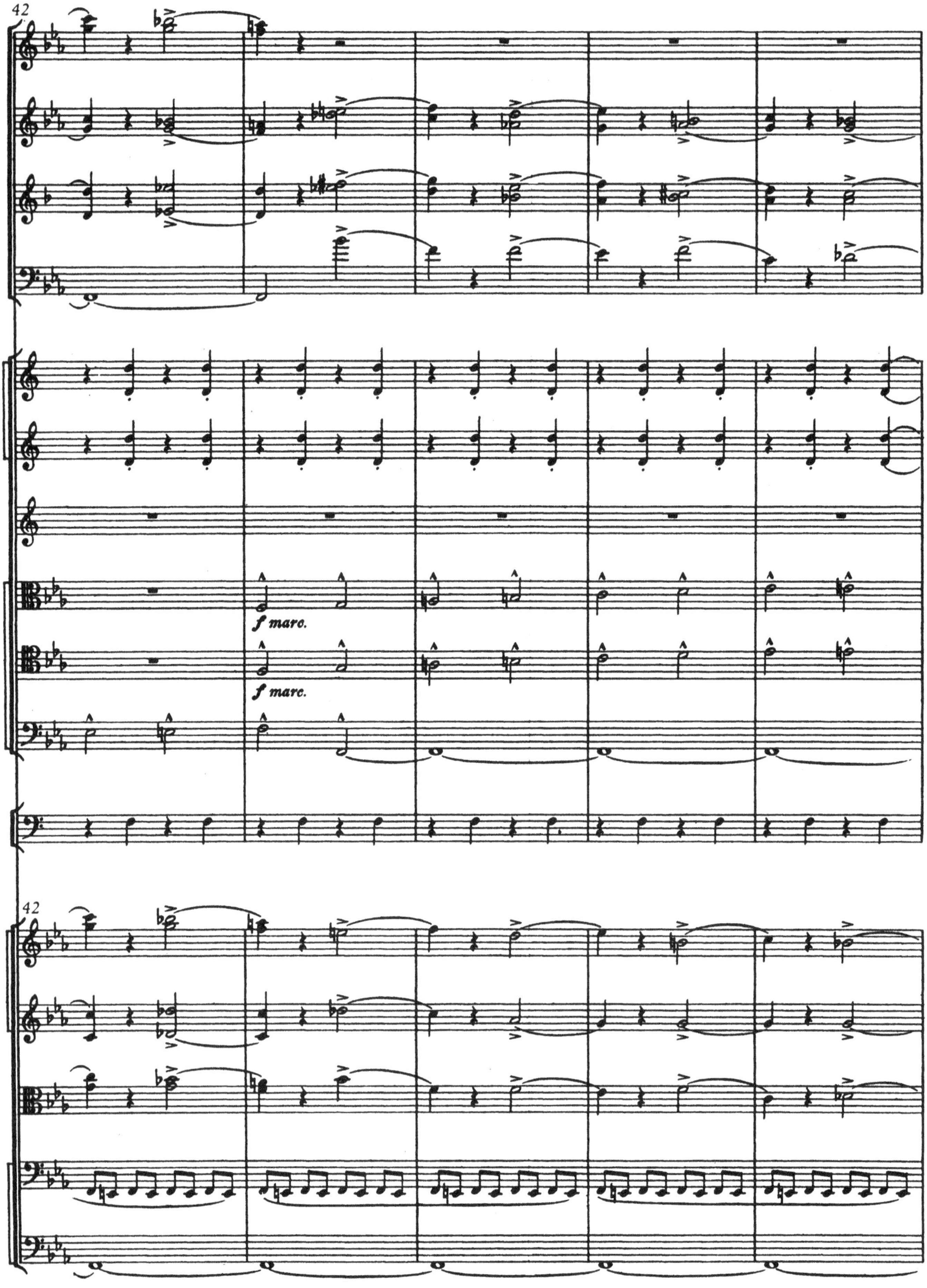
42
f marc.
f marc.
42

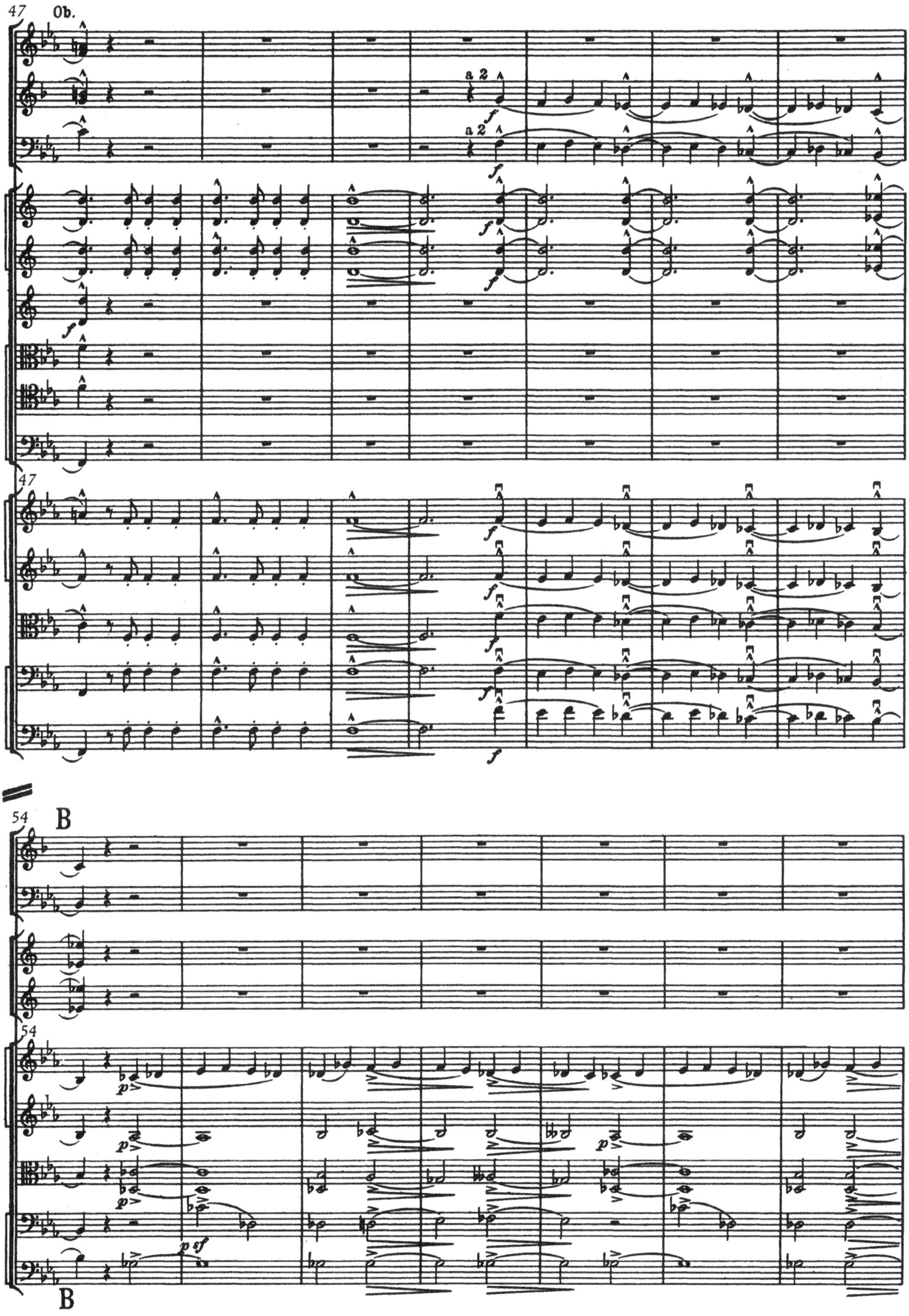
47
Ob.
a 2
a 2
f
f
f
f
47
f
f
f
f
f
54
B
54
p
p
p
p
p sf
p
B

61
a 2
p
cresc. poco a poco
a 2
cresc. poco a poco
p
cresc. poco a poco
p
cresc. poco a poco
p
sf
cresc. poco a poco
p
sf
61
div.
p cresc. poco a poco
p cresc. poco a poco
p sf
p cresc. poco a poco
p sf
p cresc. poco a poco
p cresc. poco a poco

C
68
a 2
cresc. poco a poco
mf cresc. poco a poco
mf cresc. poco a poco
68
div.
div.
C

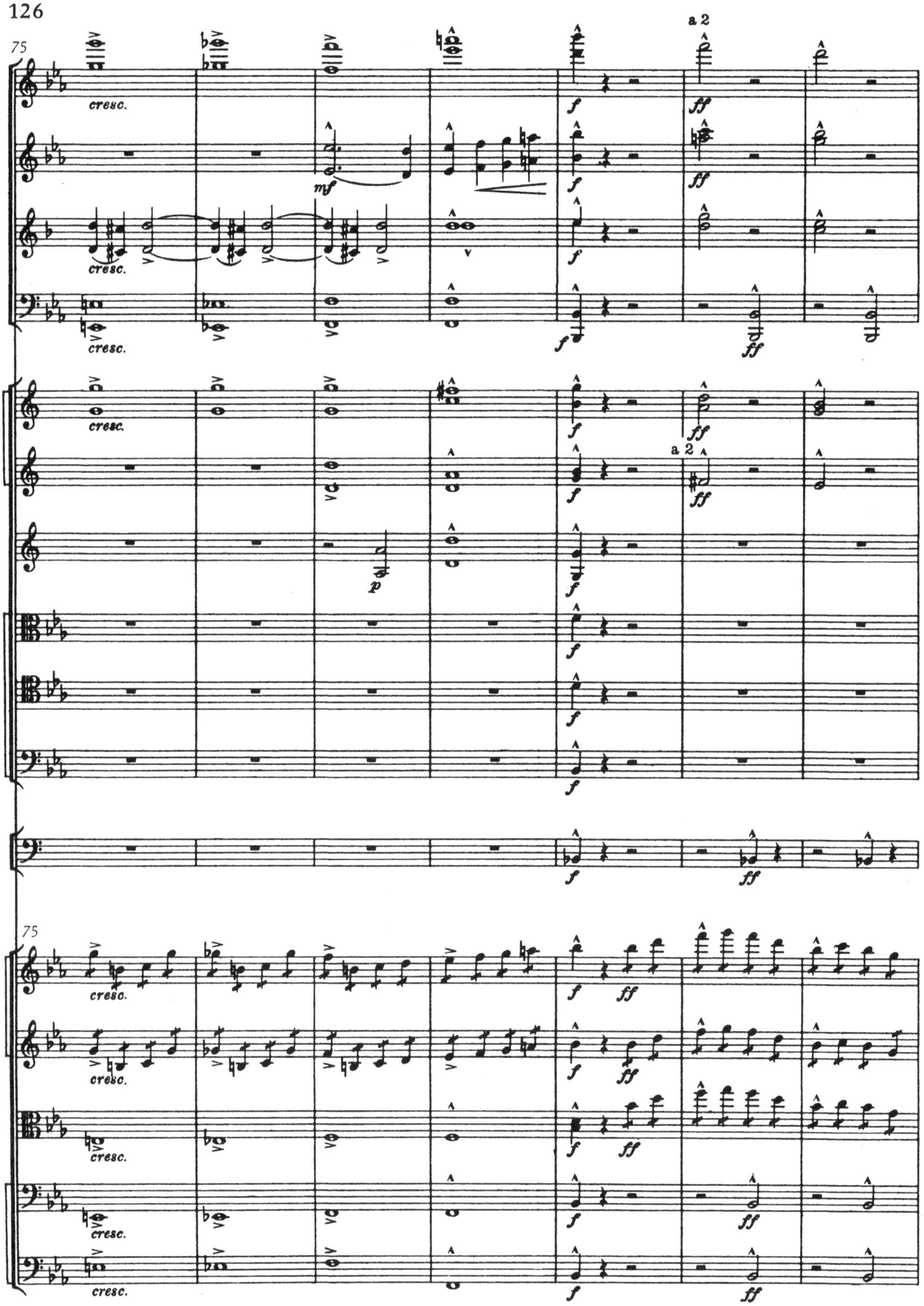
75
cresc.
a 2
f
ff
mf
p

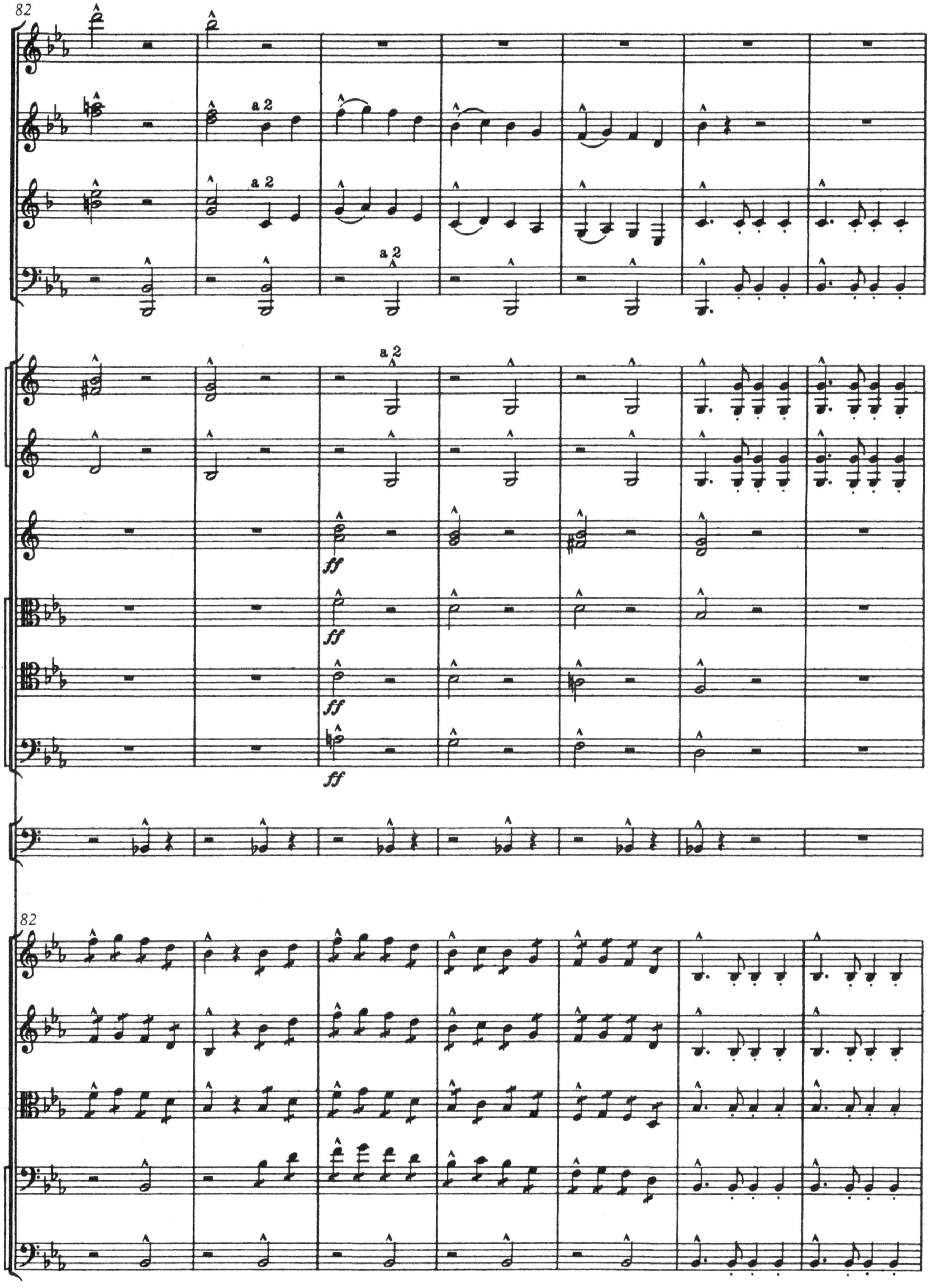
82
a 2
a 2
a 2
a 2
ff
ff
ff
ff
82

128

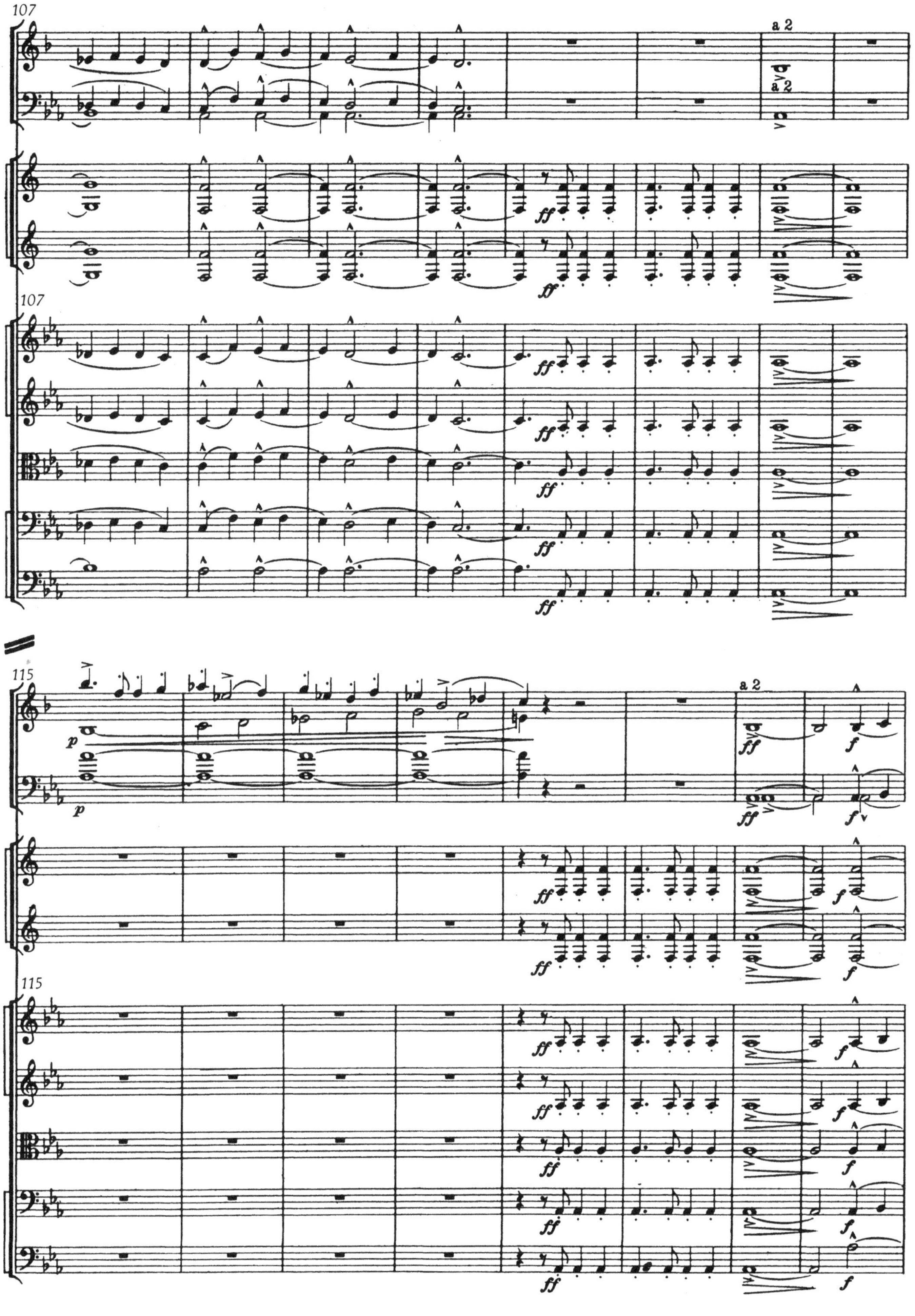
107
a 2
a 2
107
ff
115
p
a 2
ff
f
115
ff
f

123
Fl.
D
p
cresc. poco a poco
p
cresc. poco a poco
Trbne I
mf marc.
123
D
130
a 2
Ob.
p cresc.
Trbni.
mf marc.
mf marc.
mf cresc.
mf cresc.
mf
130

137
a 2
marc.
a 2
marc.
marc.
a 2
marc.
ff
137
ff marc.
ff marc.
ff marc.
ff marc.
ff

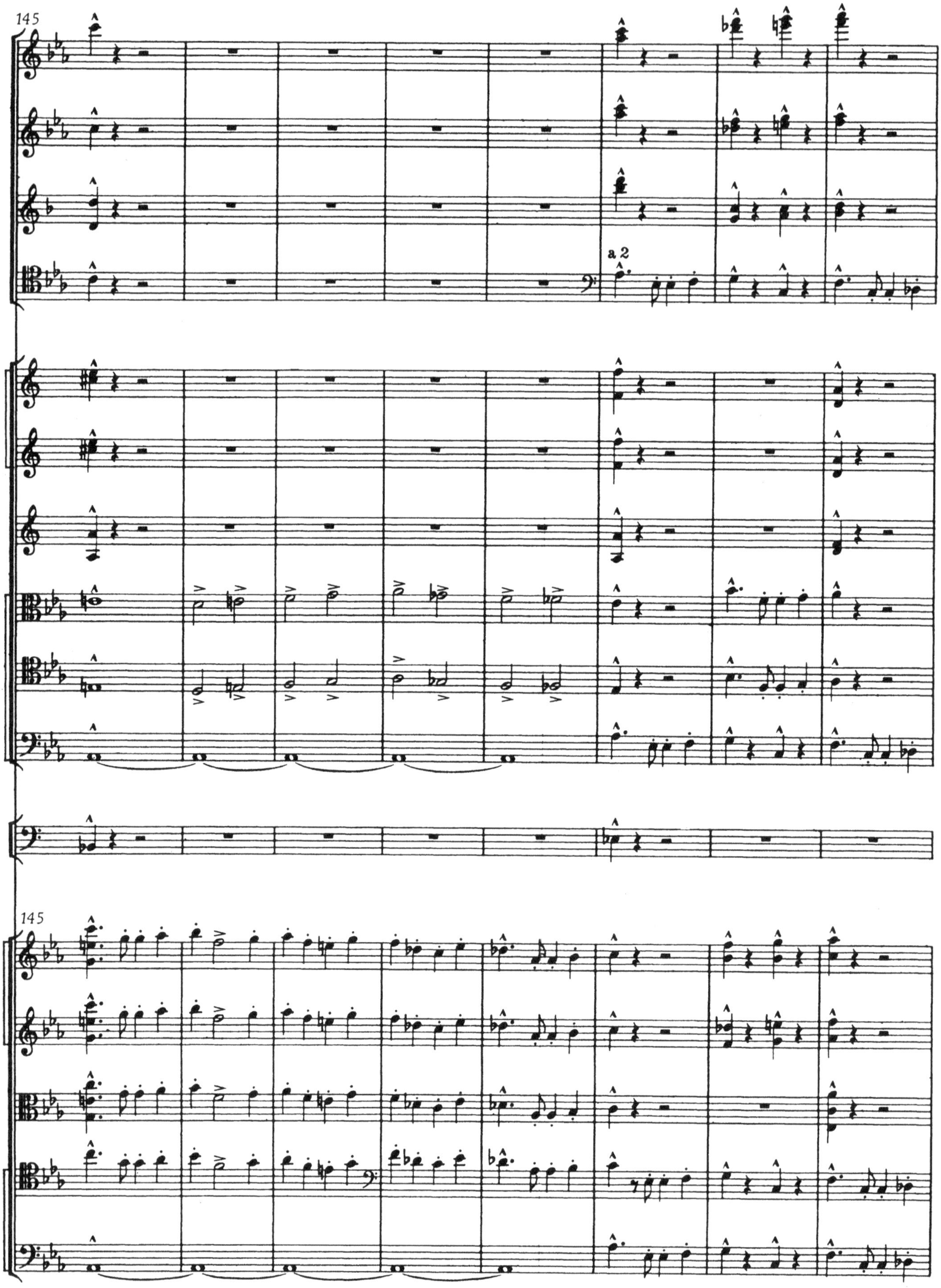
145
a 2
145

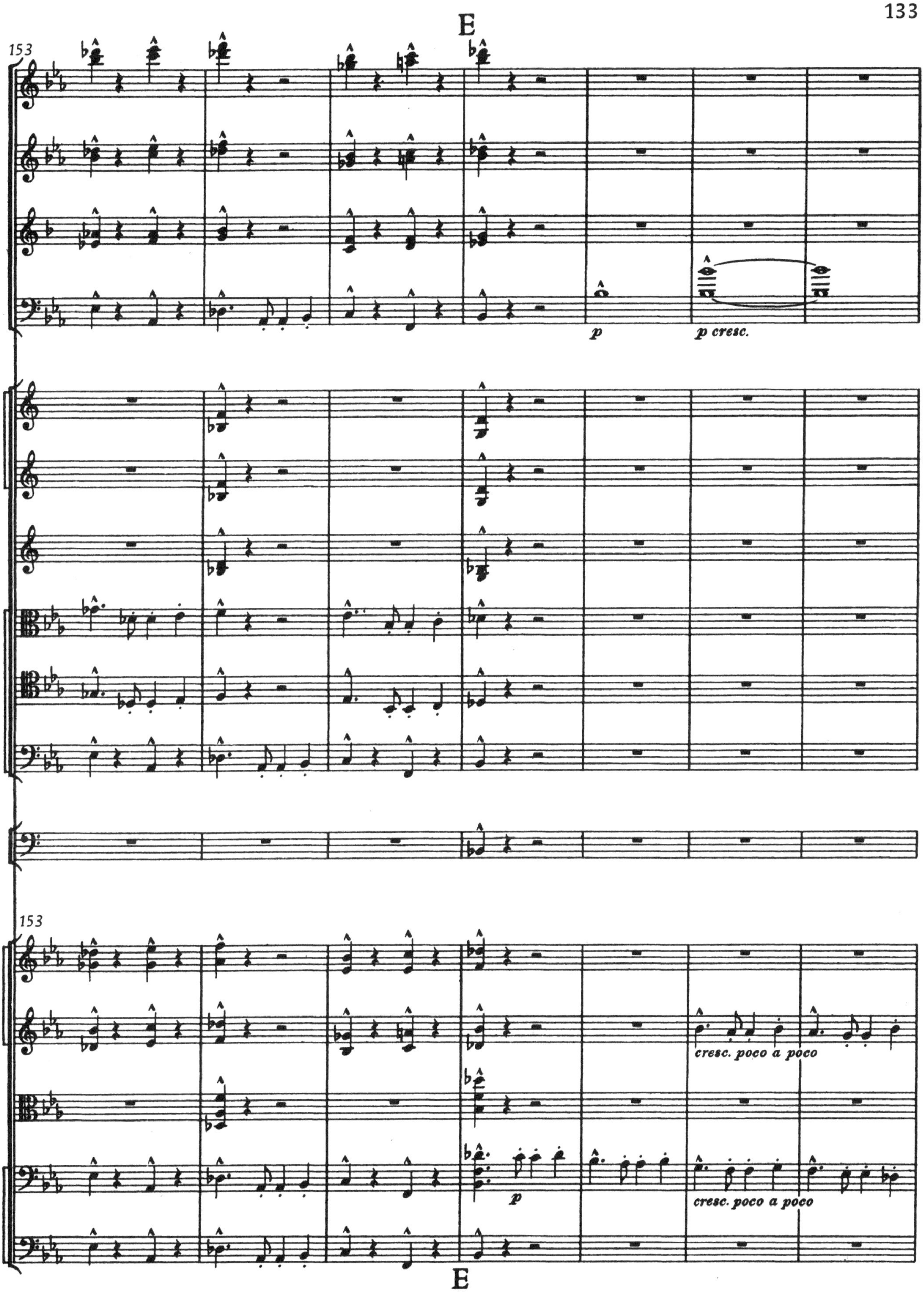
E
153
p
p cresc.
153
cresc. poco a poco
p
cresc. poco a poco
E

160
mf cresc.
a2
f
mf cresc.
f
p cresc.
mf cresc.
a2
f
mf cresc.
f
a2
f
160
p cresc.
mf cresc.
f
mf cresc.
f
p cresc.
mf cresc.
f
mf cresc.
f
mf cresc.
f

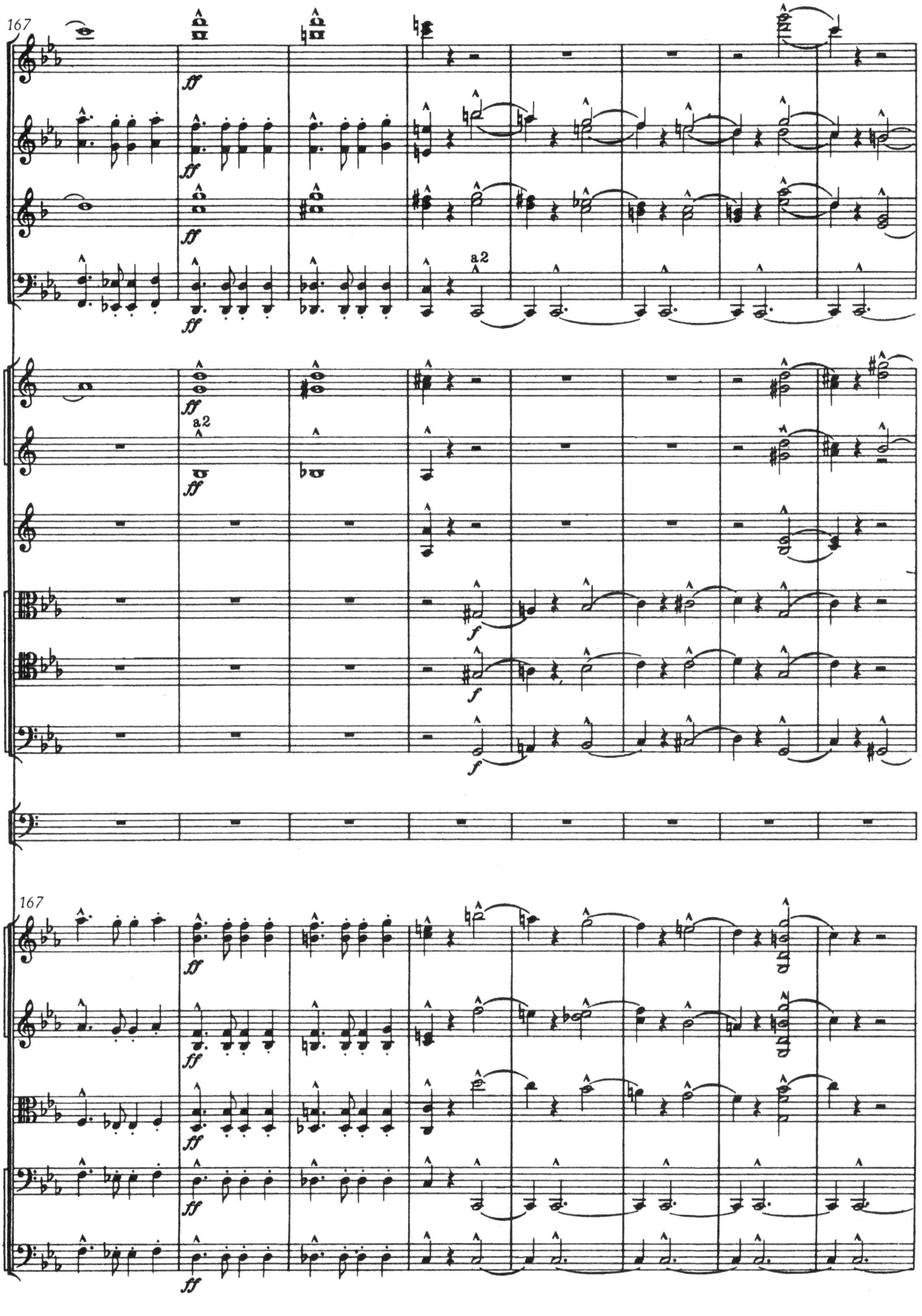
167
ff
a2
f
167

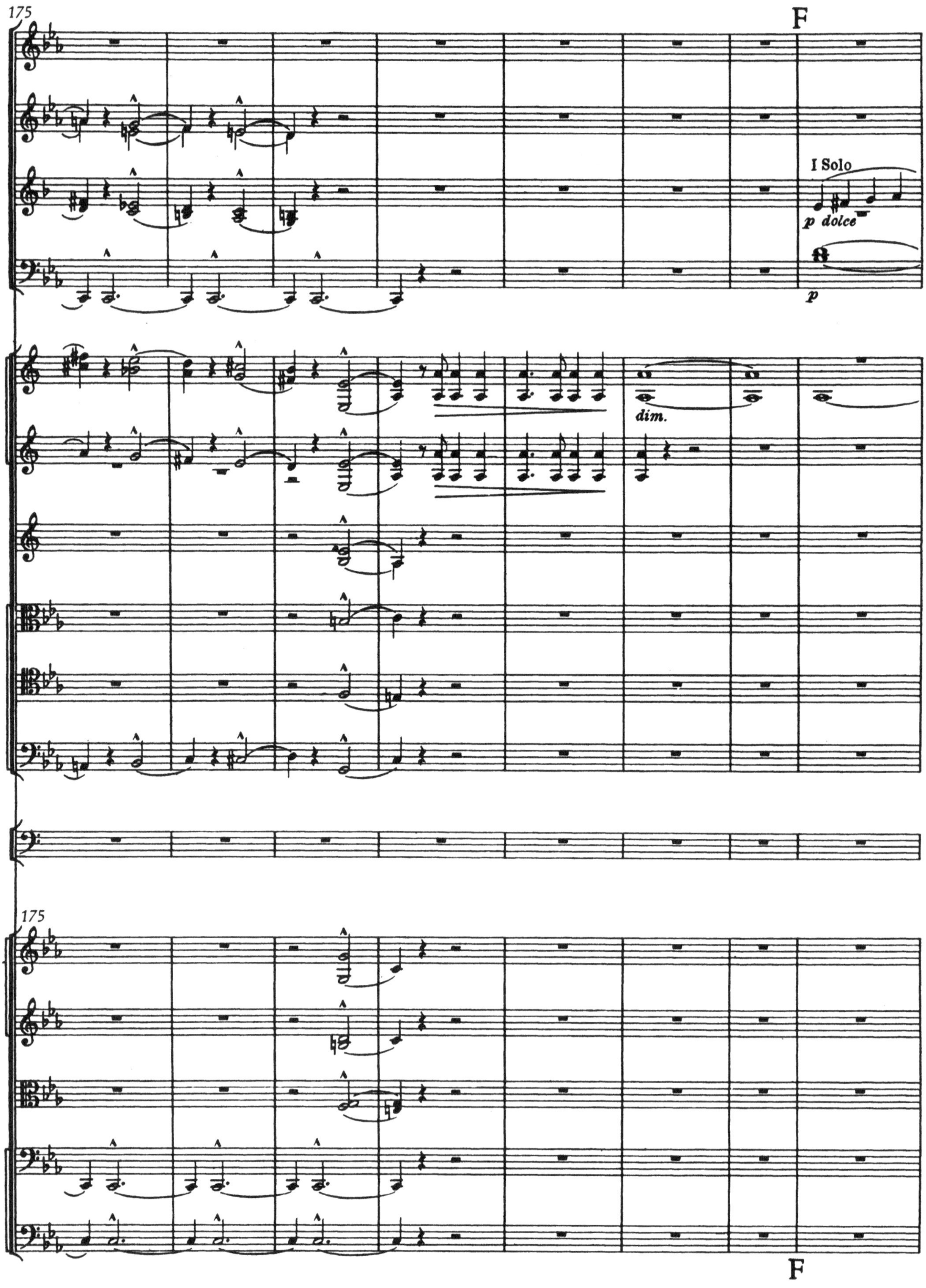
175
F
I Solo
p dolce
p
dim.
175
F

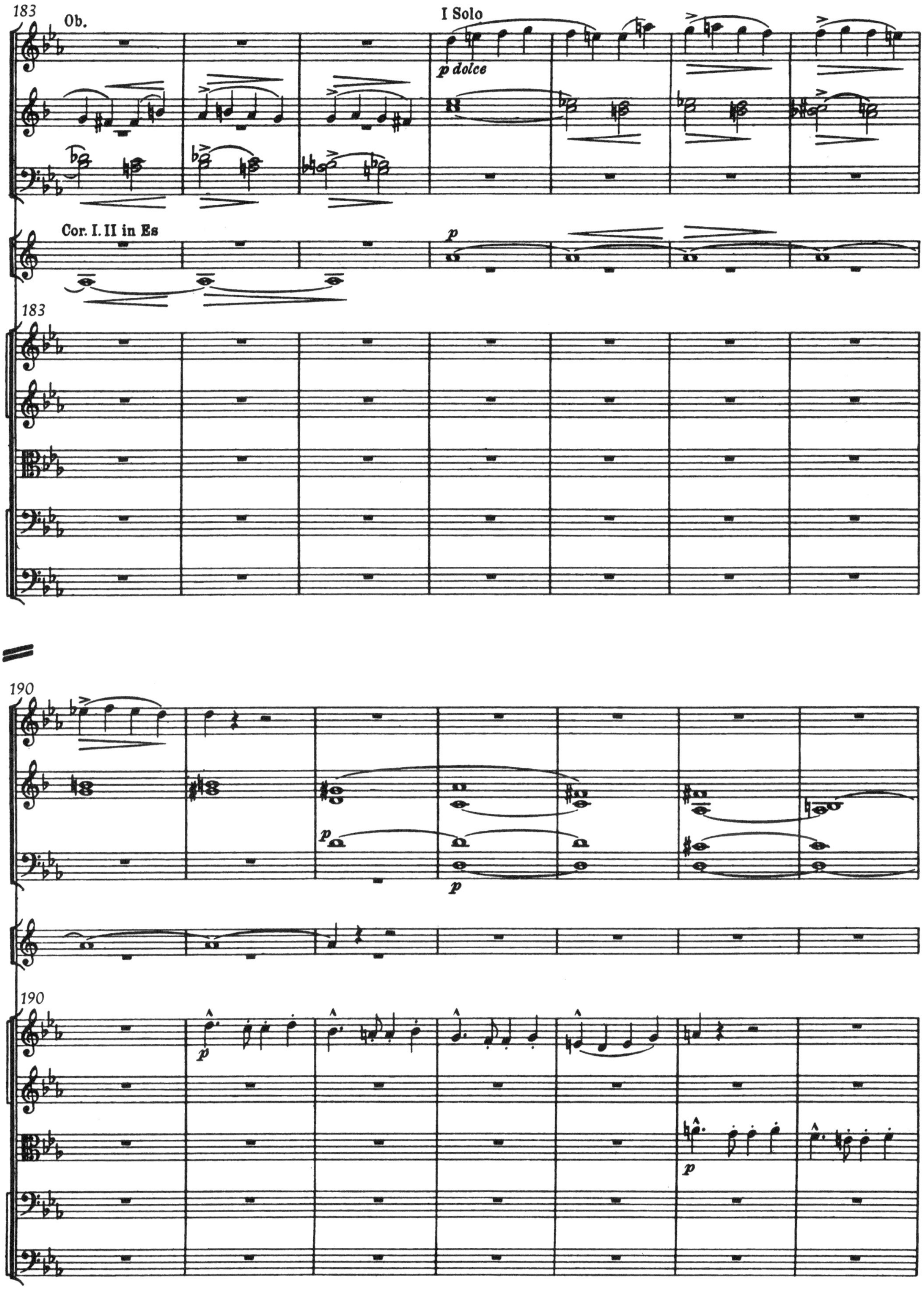
183
Ob.
I Solo
p dolce
Cor. I. II in Es
p
183
190
p
p
190
p
p

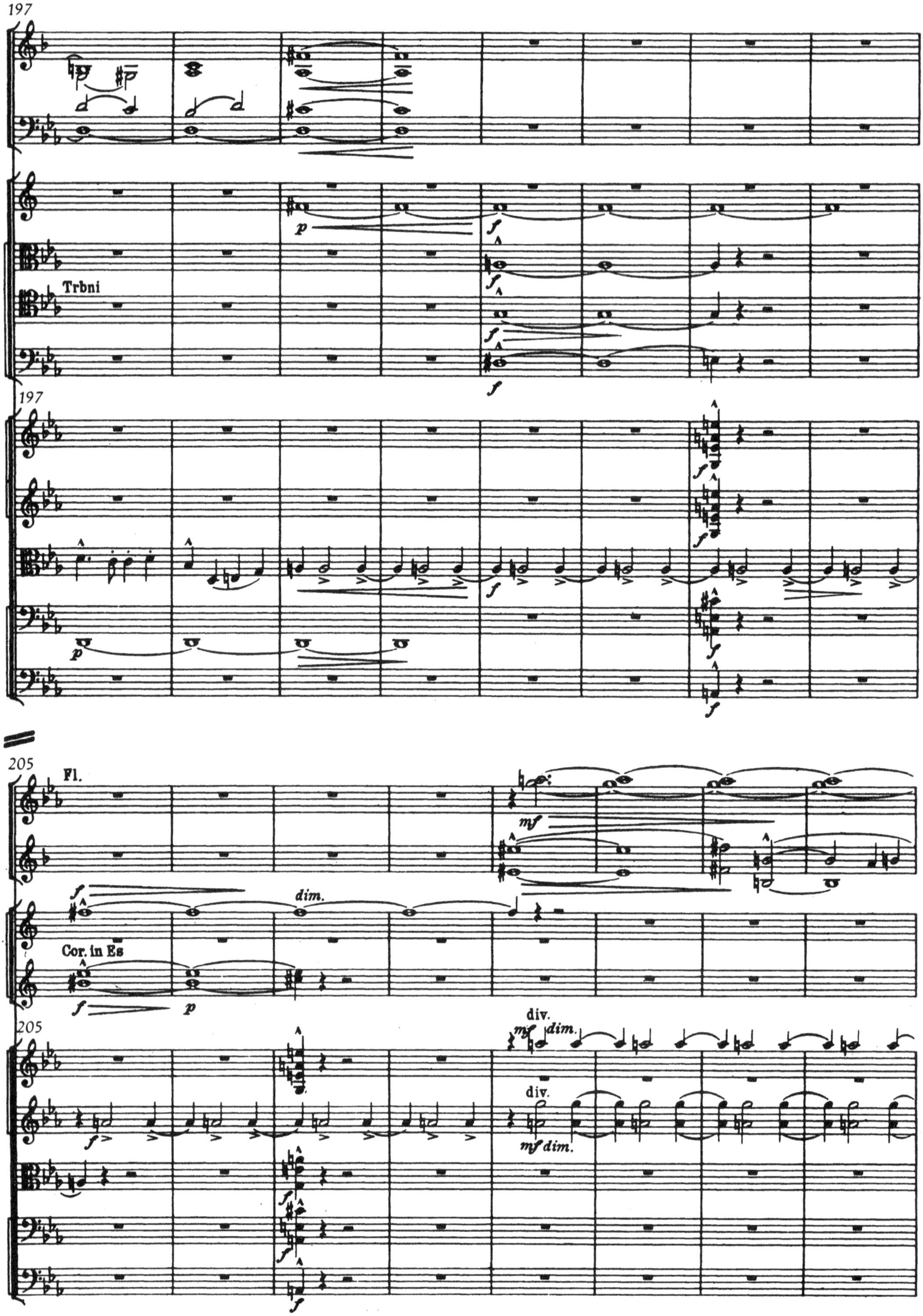
197
Trbni
197
205
Fl.
dim.
Cor. in Es
205
div.
div.
mf dim.

G
213
Ob.
a 2
p
f marc.
f marc.
Fag.
a 2
p
p
f marc.
a 2
f marc.
213
p
arco
f
pizz.
marc.
p
pizz.
f marc.
pizz.
f marc.
pizz.
mf
f marc.
G
220
p
a 2
f marc.
a 2
f marc.
p
a 2
f marc.
220

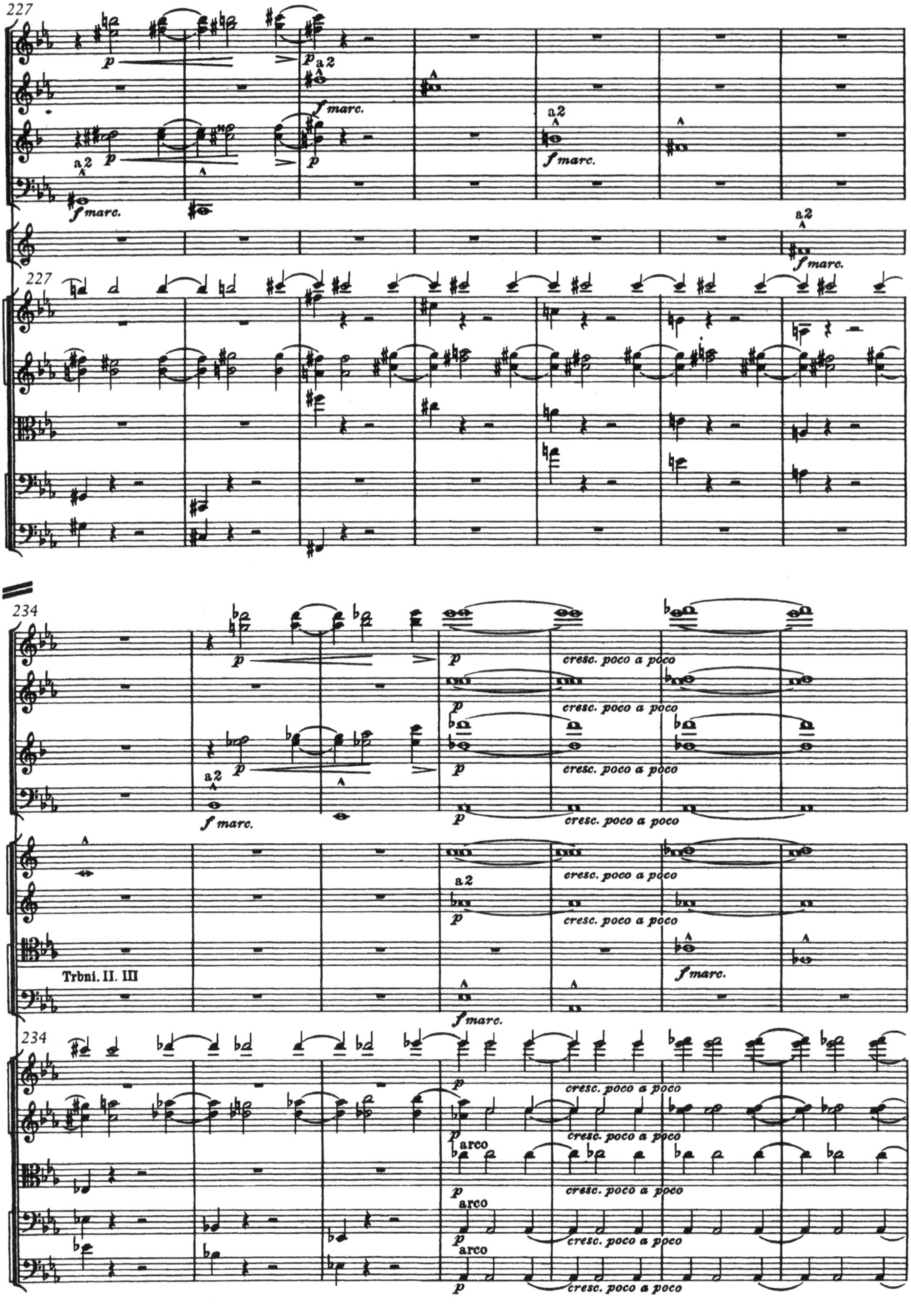
227
p
a 2
f marc.
234
cresc. poco a poco
Trbni. II. III
arco

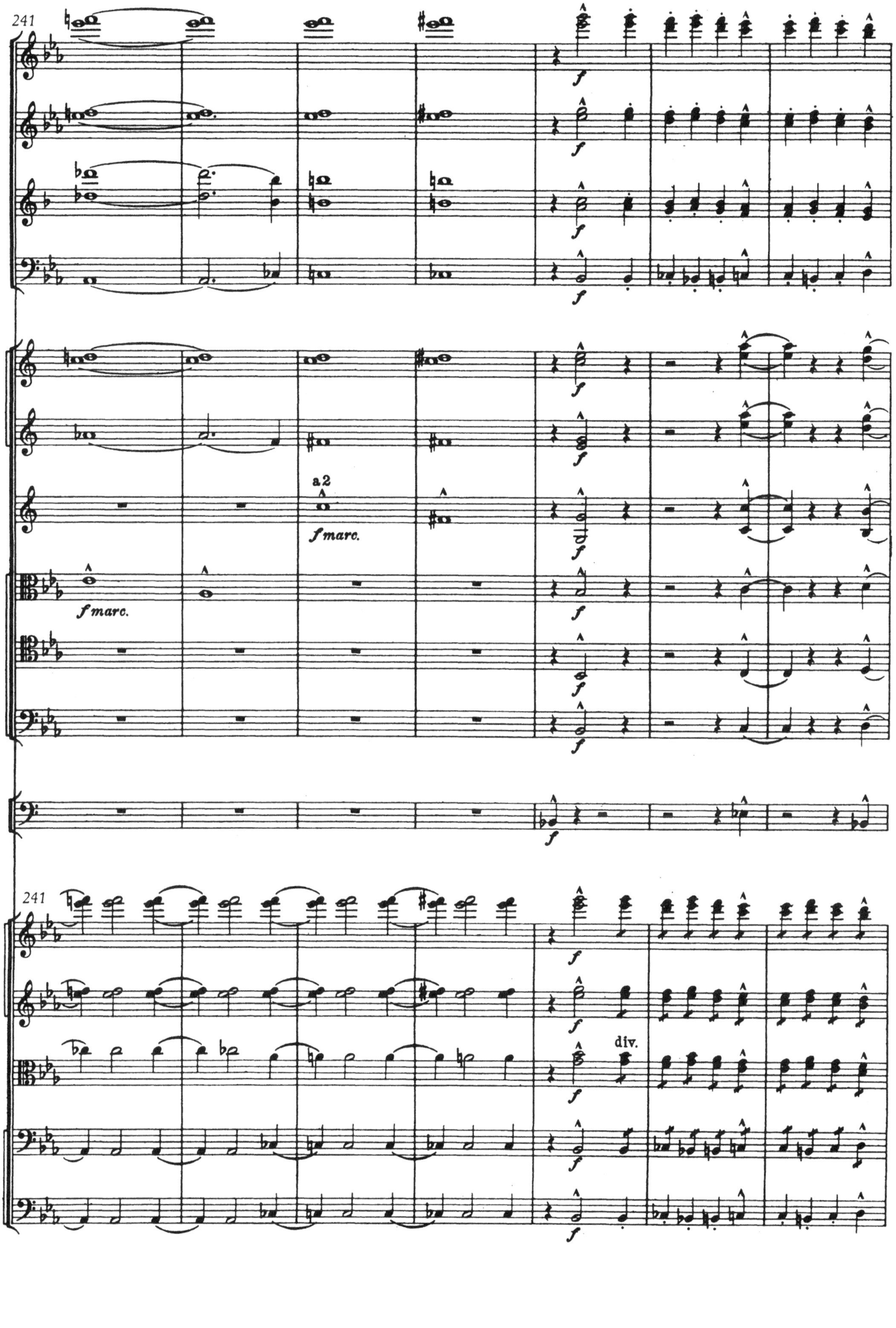
241
a 2
f marc.
f marc.
241
div.

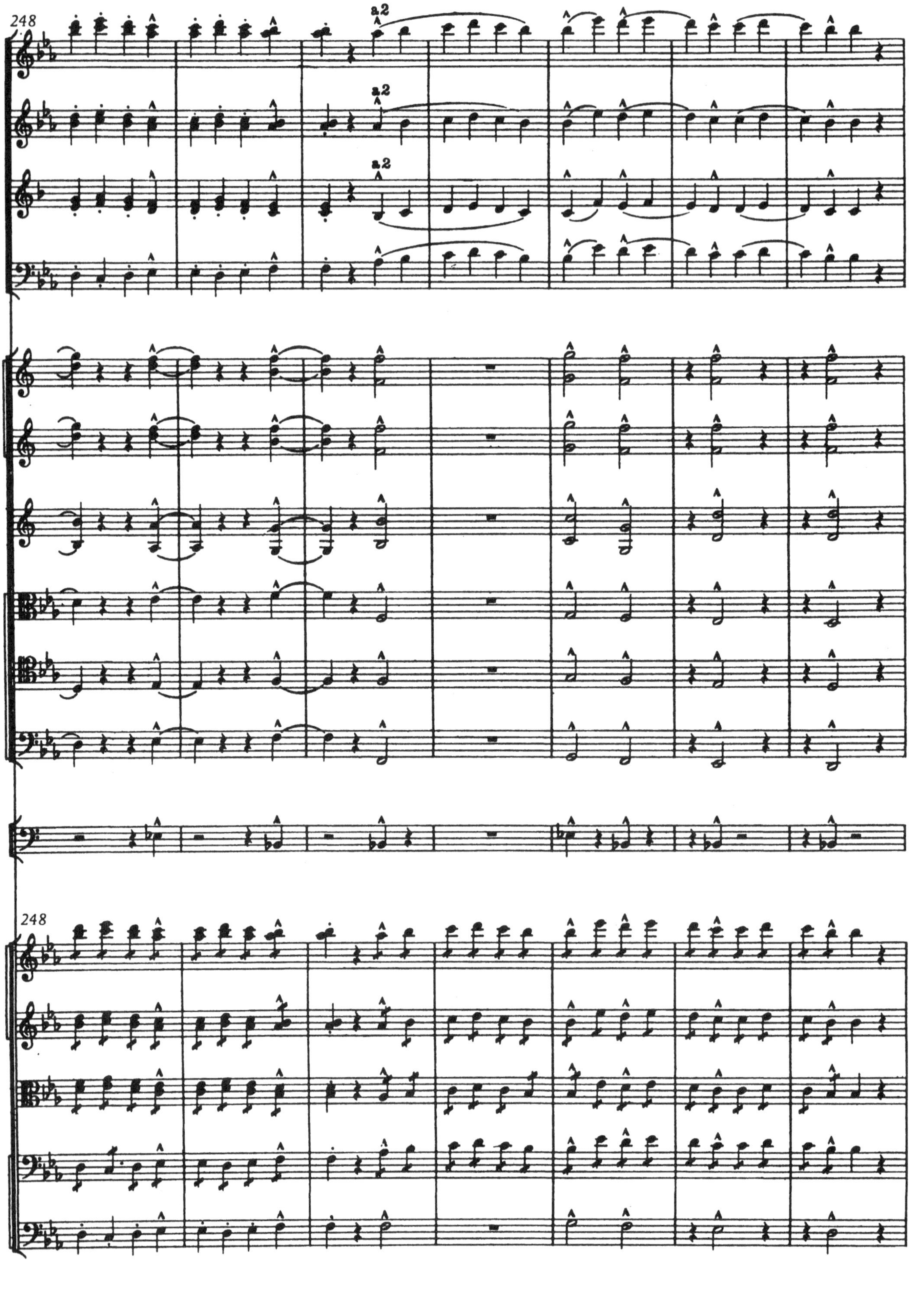
248
a2
a2
a2
248

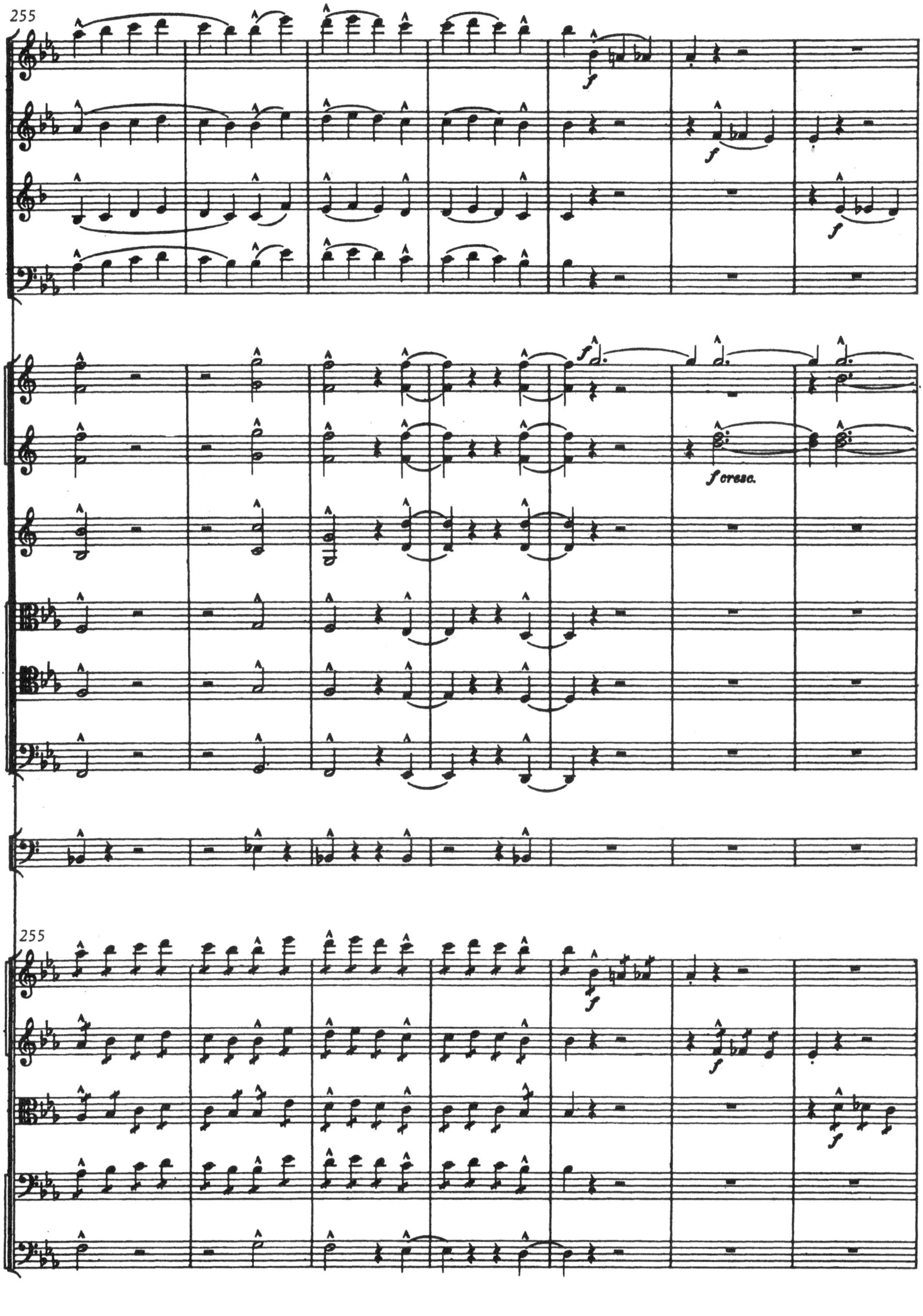
255
f
f
f
f
f cresc.
255
f
f
f

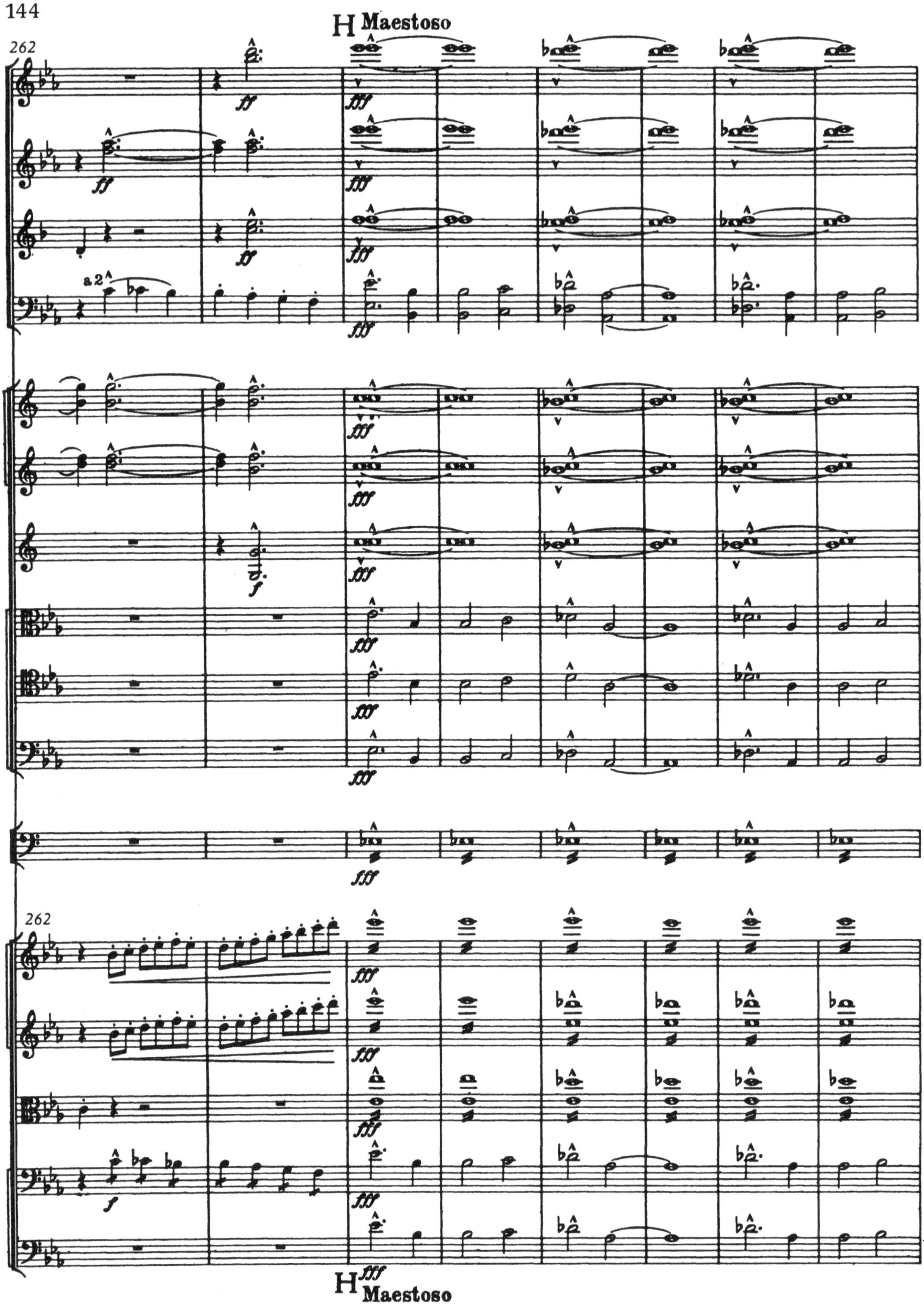
H Maestoso
262
a 2
ff
fff
f
H
Maestoso

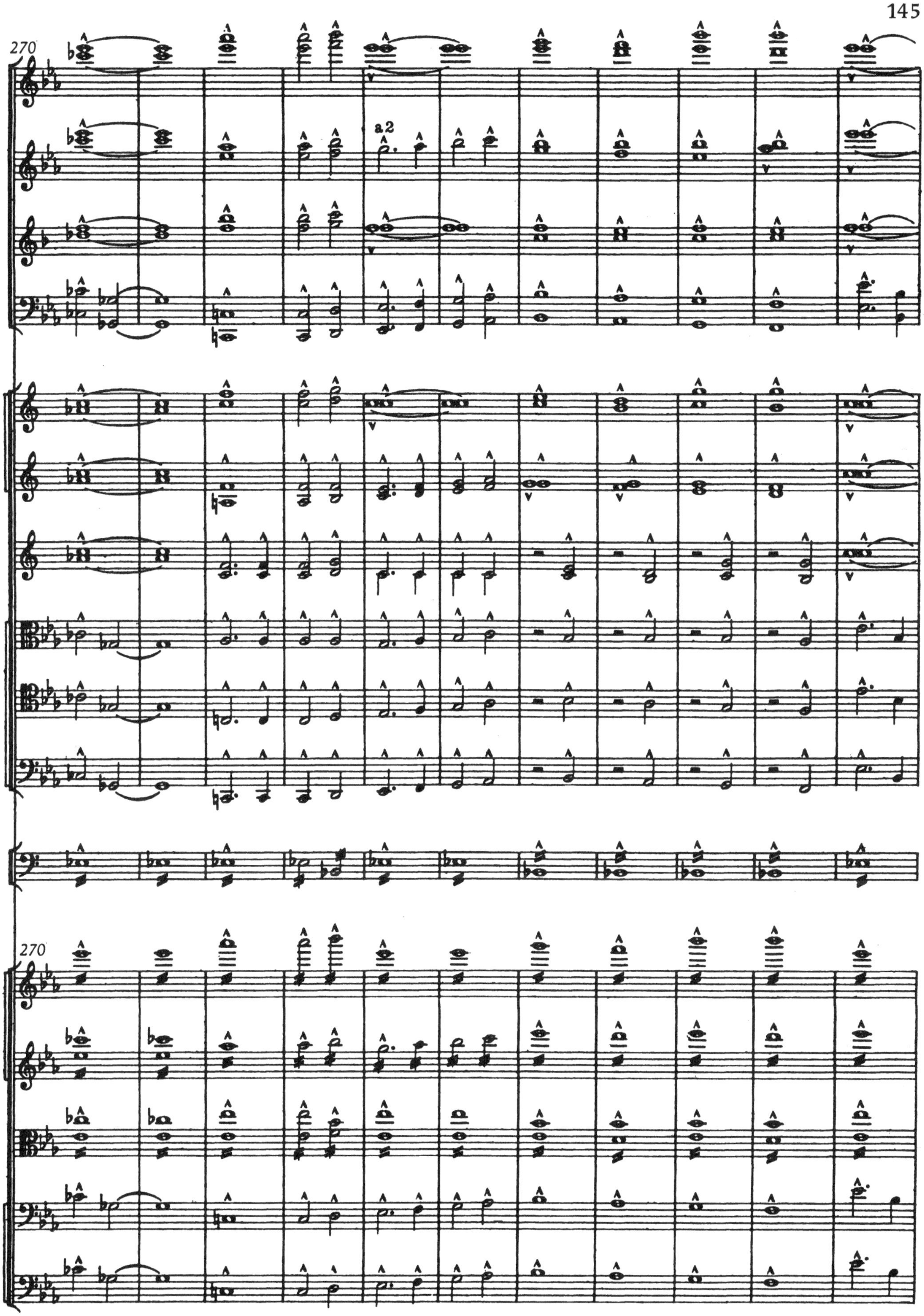
270
a 2
270

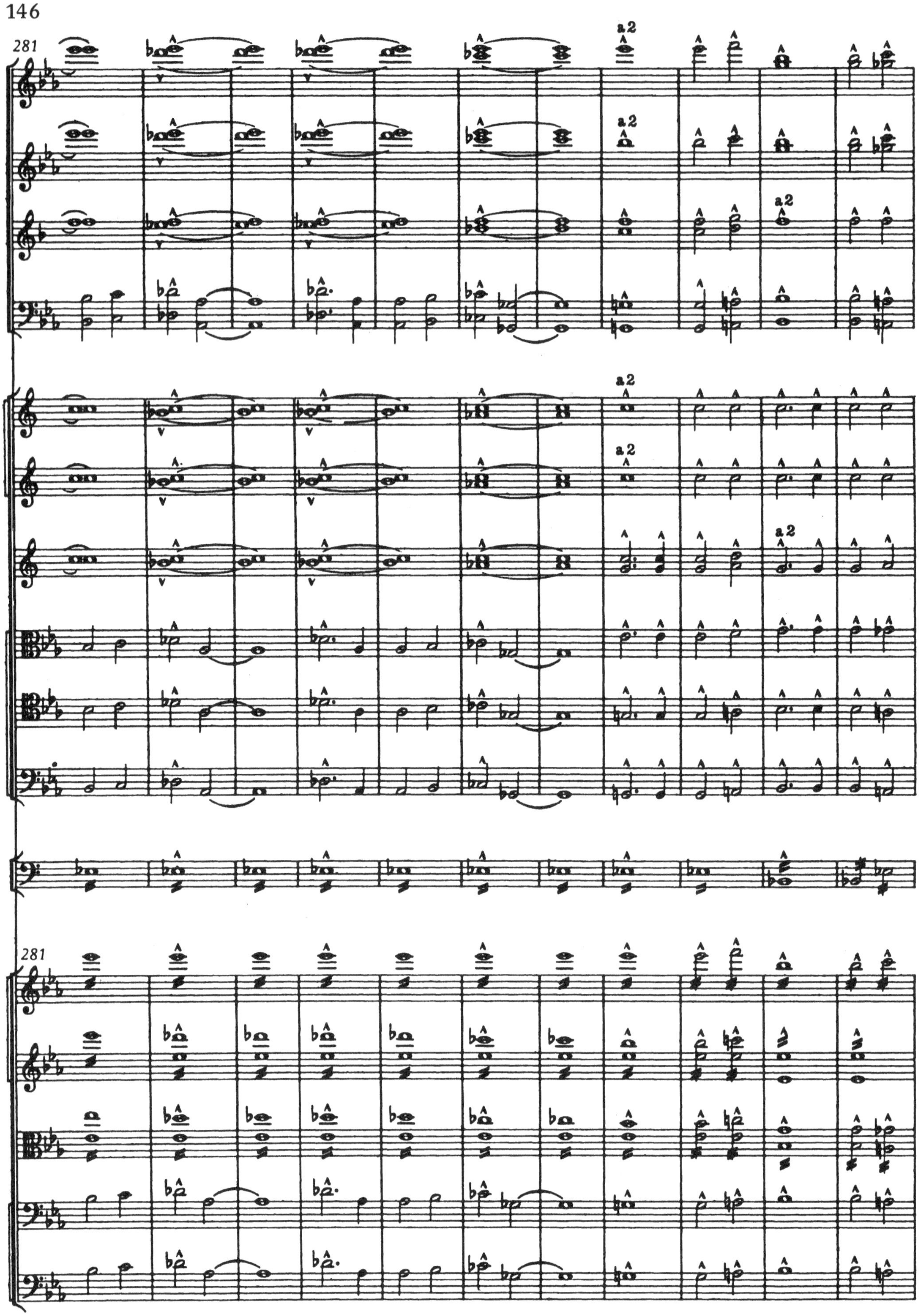
281
a 2
a 2
a 2
a 2
a 2
a 2
281

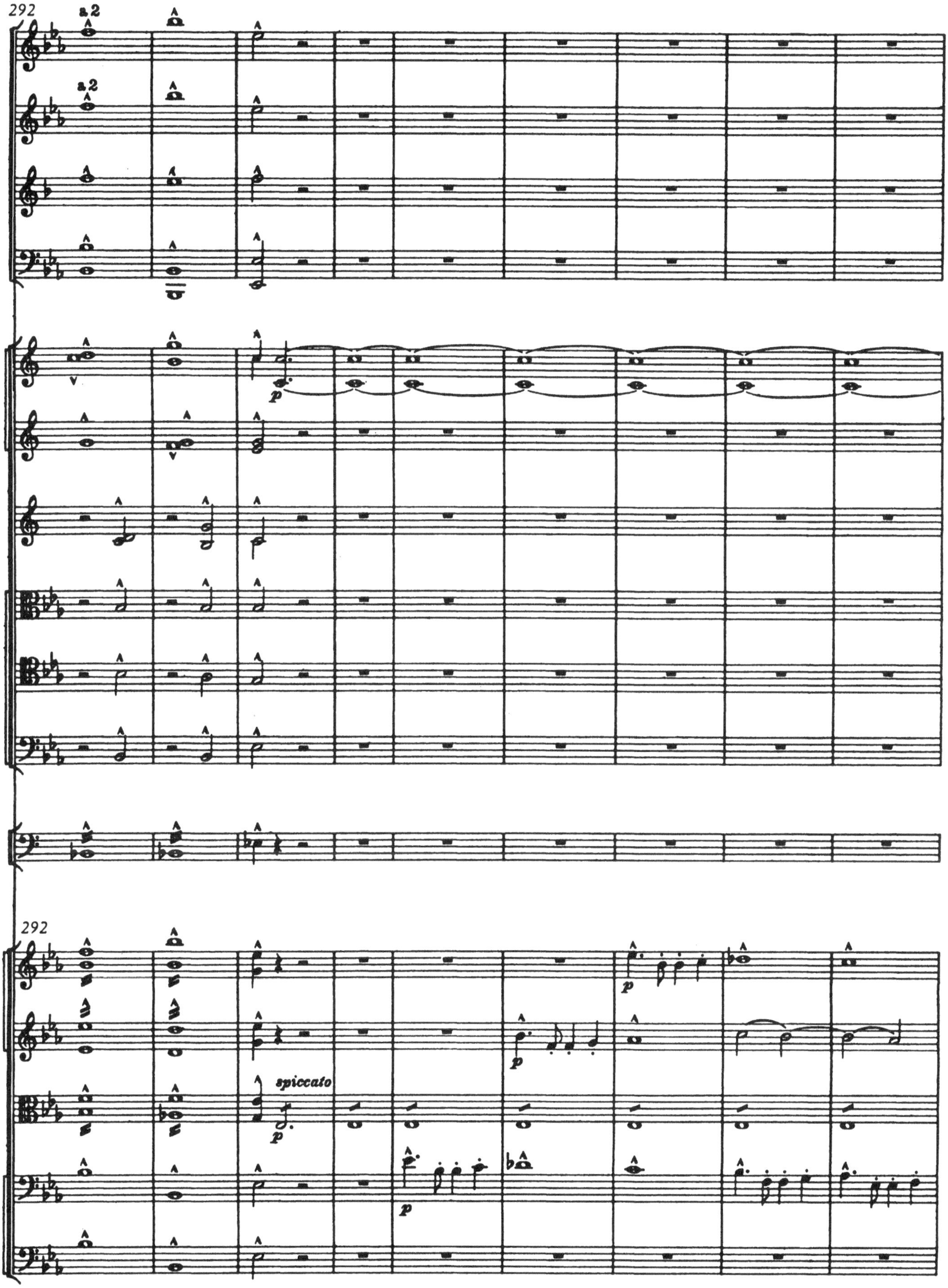
292
a 2
a 2
p
292
p
spiccato
p
p
p

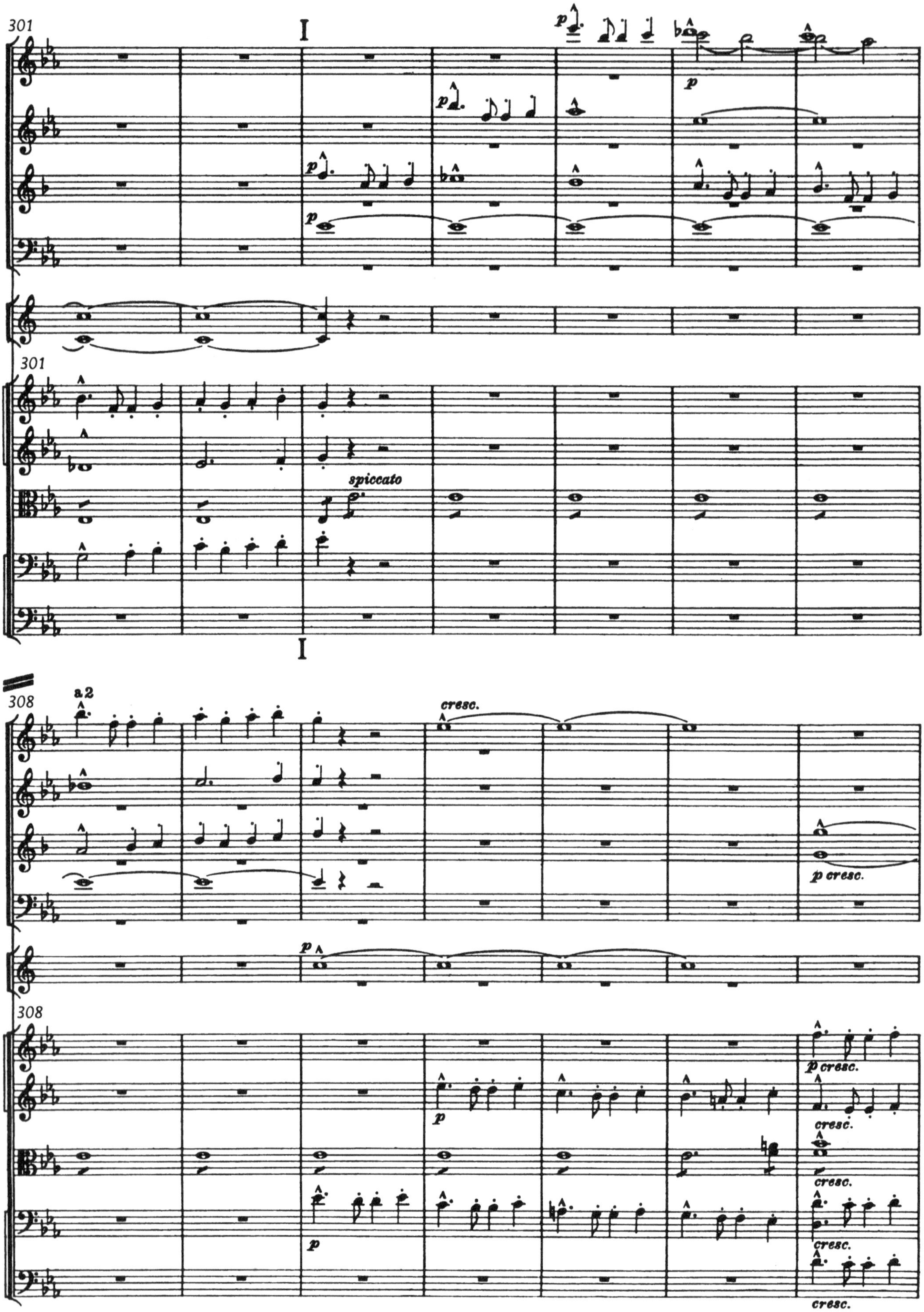
301
I
p
spiccato
I
308
a 2
cresc.
p cresc.
cresc.

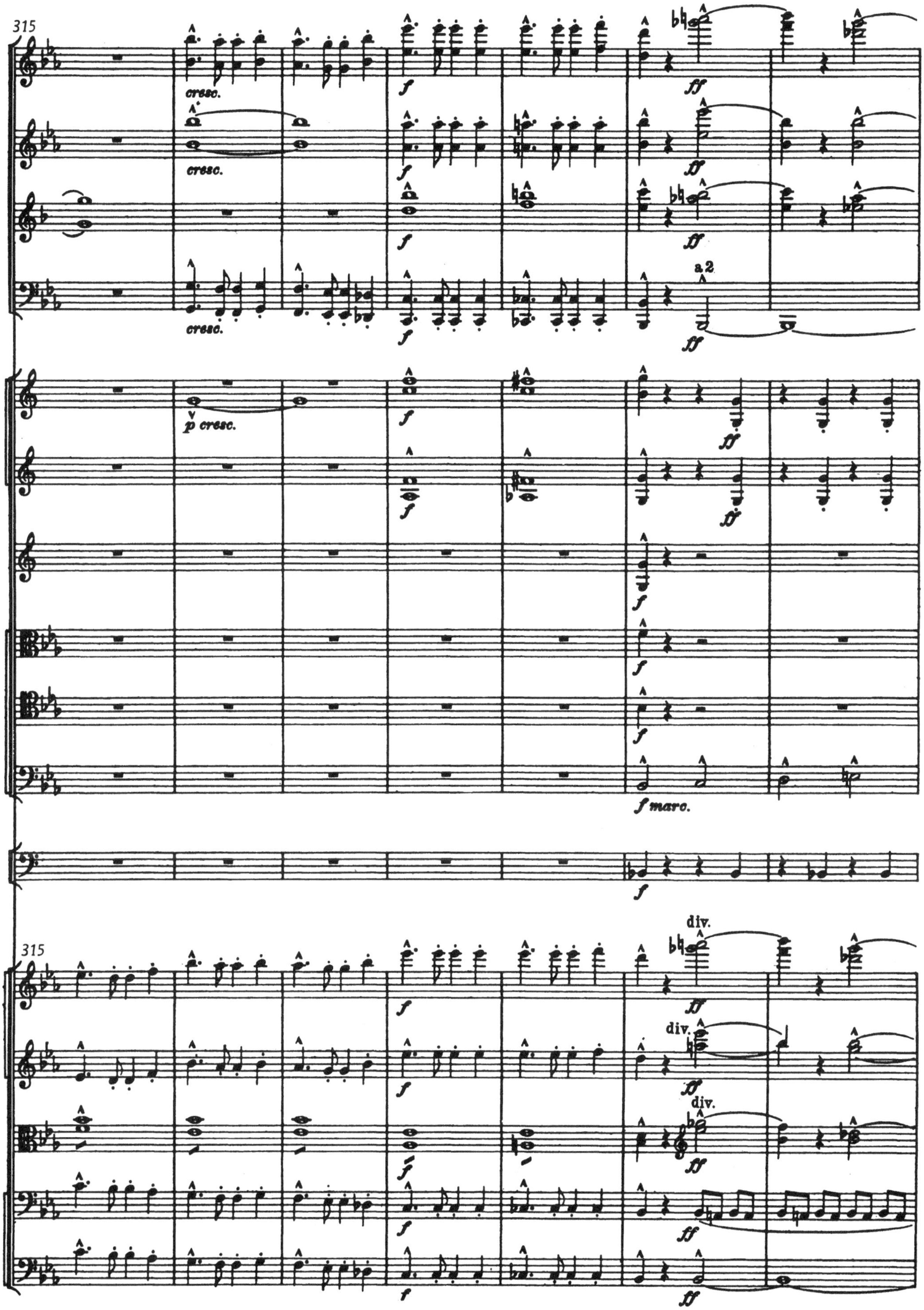
315
cresc.
f
ff
a 2
p cresc.
f marc.
div.
315

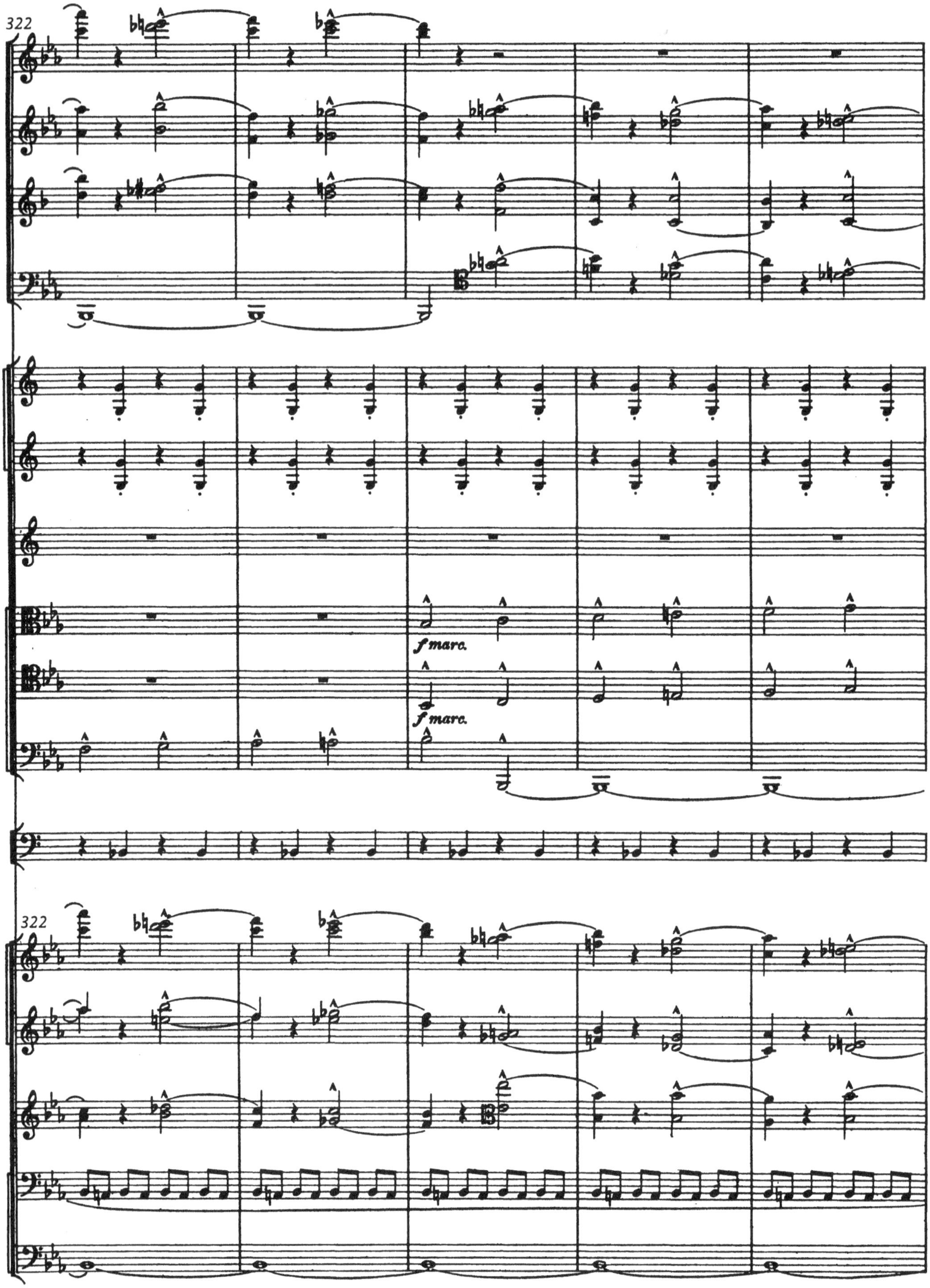
322
f marc.
f marc.
322

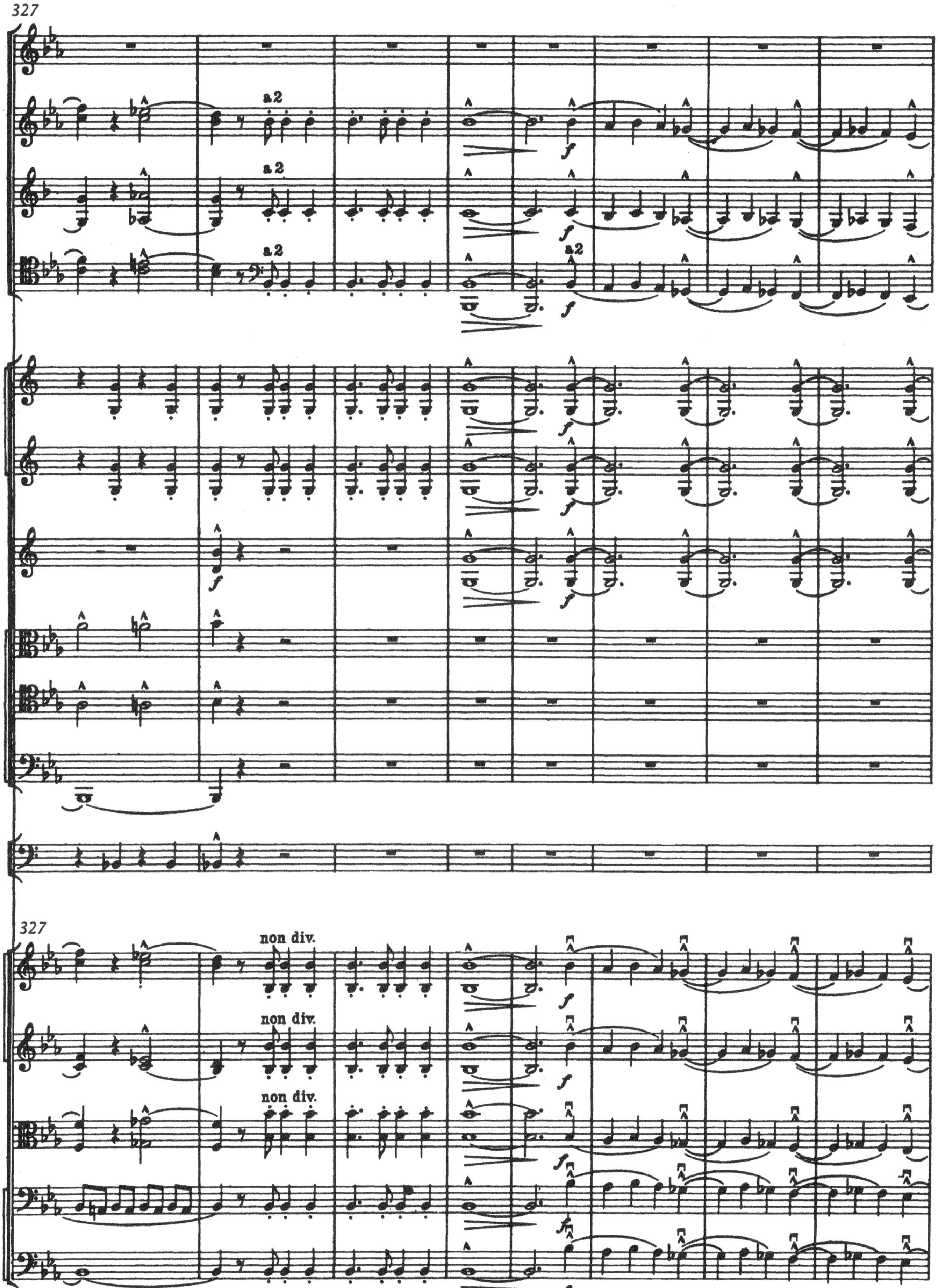
327
a 2
a 2
a 2
f
327
non div.
non div.
non div.

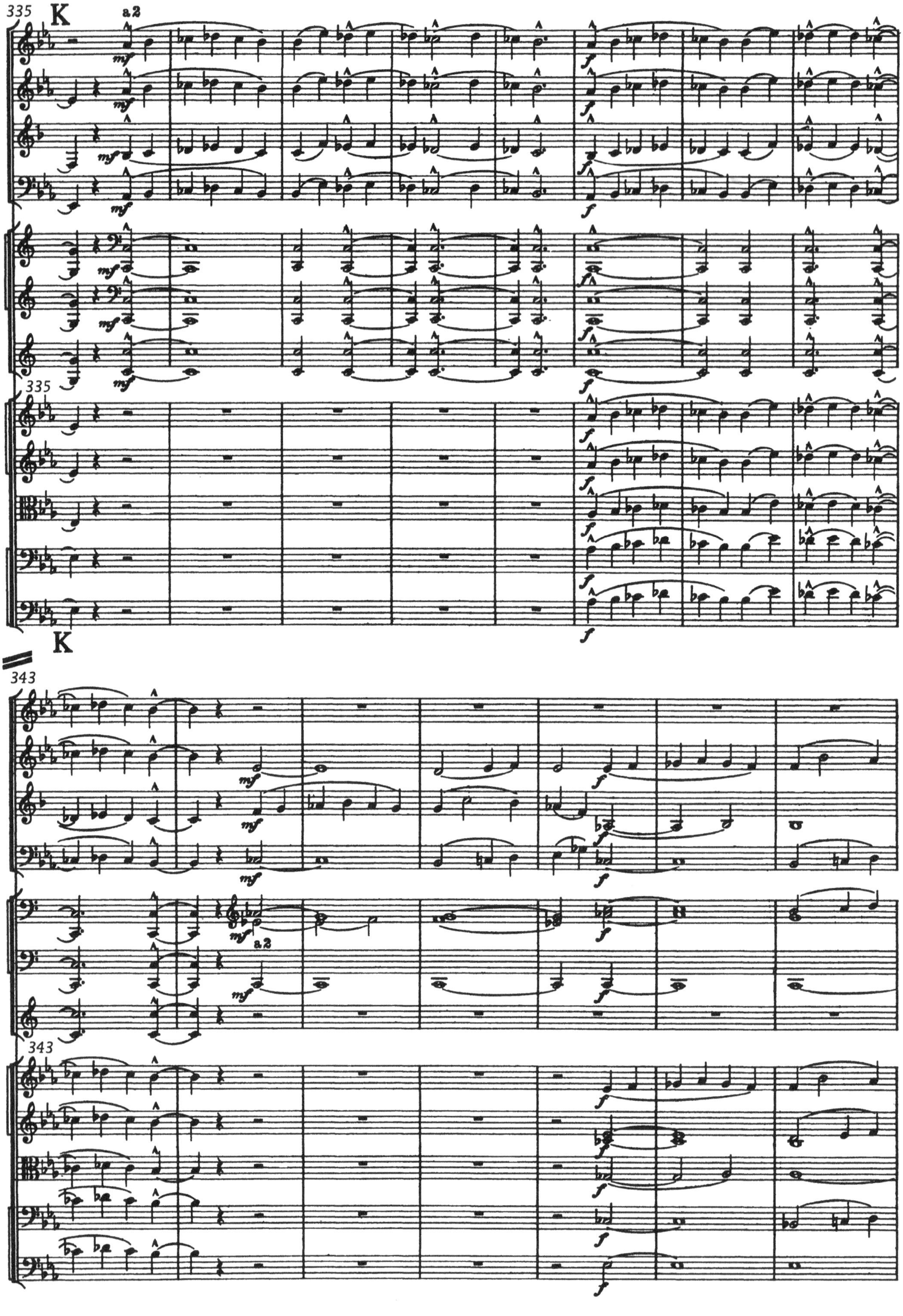
335
K
a 2
335
K
343
a 2
343

350
a 2
350
L
357
f marc.
a 2
f marc.
a 2
f marc.
Cor. I. II in Es
a 2
f marc.
357
div. pizz. marc.
p arco
div.
pizz.
f marc.
pizz.
pizz.
fp cresc. poco a poco
L

365
p
a 2
f marc.
a 2
p
a 2
f marc.
a 2
f marc.
365
arco
p
pizz.
mf
373
a 2
f marc.
a 2
f marc.
p
p
a 2
f marc.
f marc.
373
arco
p
pizz.
mf

381
p
p
p
p
a 2
f marc.
f marc.
p
f marc.
381
non div.
arco
f marc.
arco
f marc.
f
p
arco
p
f
p
389
Ob.
cresc. poco a poco
a 2
cresc. poco a poco
p
f marc.
p
cresc. poco a poco
Cor. III. IV in Es
p
cresc. poco a poco
mf marc.
mf marc.
mf marc.
p
cresc. poco a poco
389
cresc. poco a poco
cresc. poco a poco
f
p
cresc. poco a poco
f
p
cresc. poco a poco

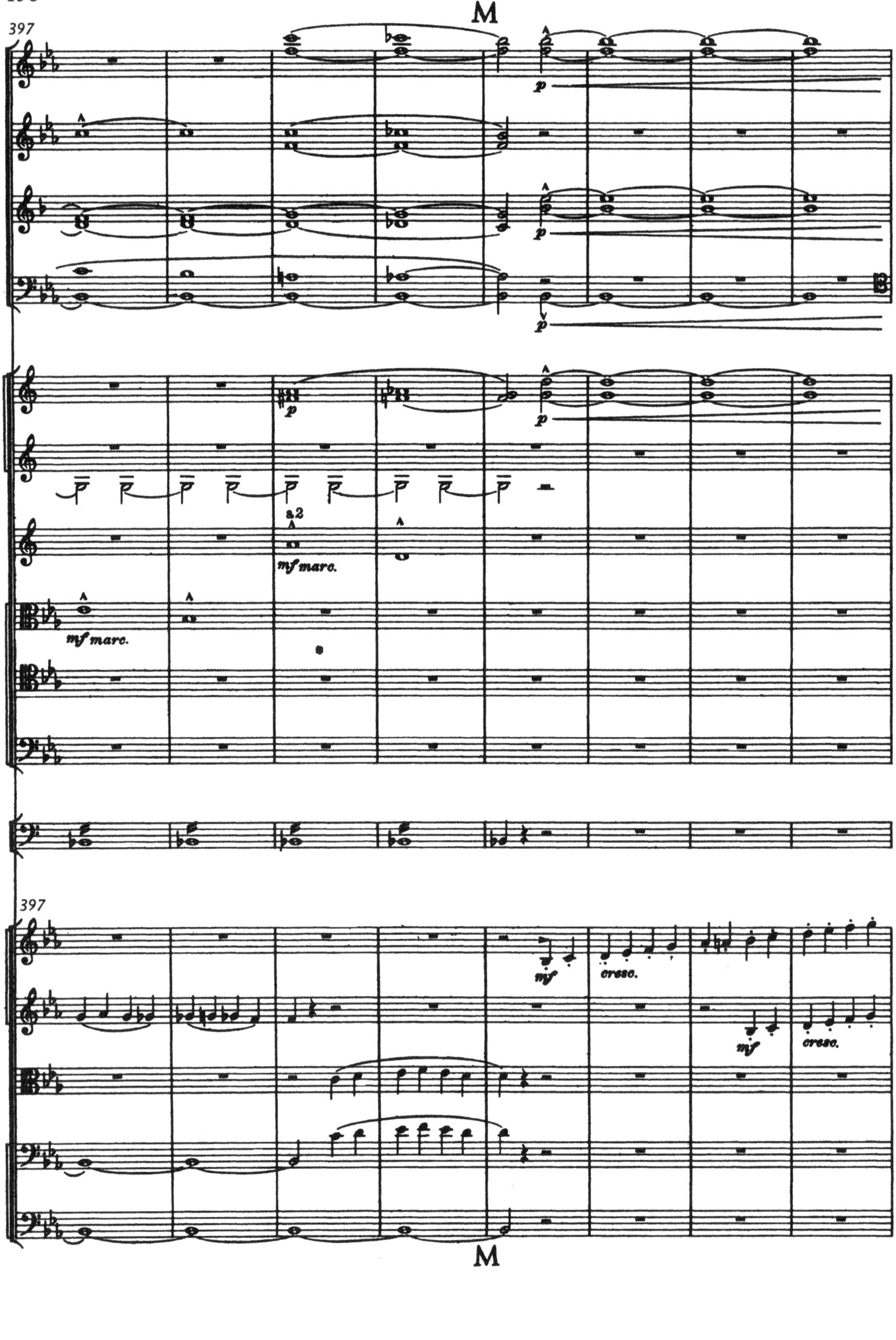
M
397
p
p
p
p
p
a 2
mf marc.
mf marc.
397
mf
cresc.
mf
cresc.
M

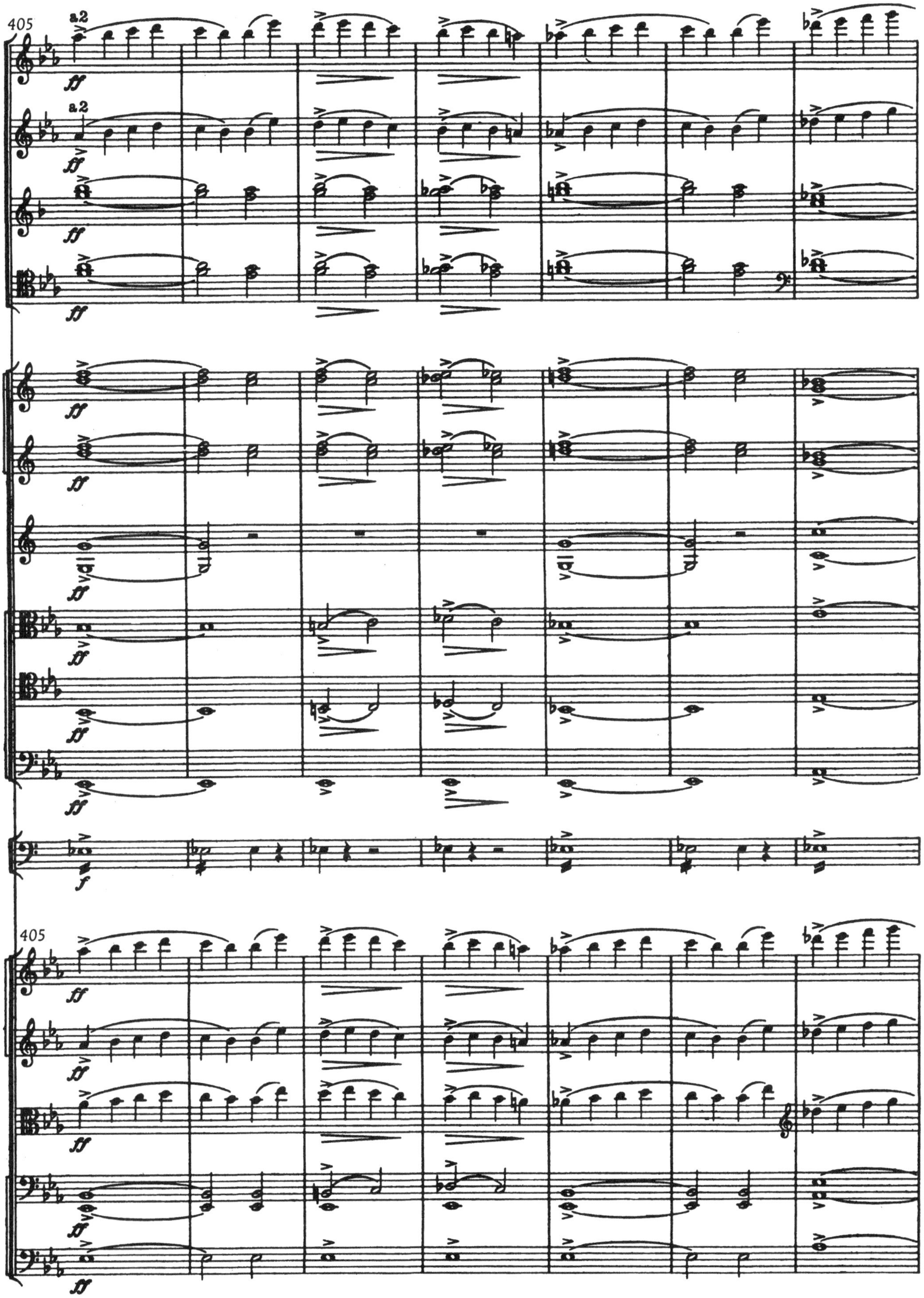
405
a2
ff
a2
ff
f
405
ff

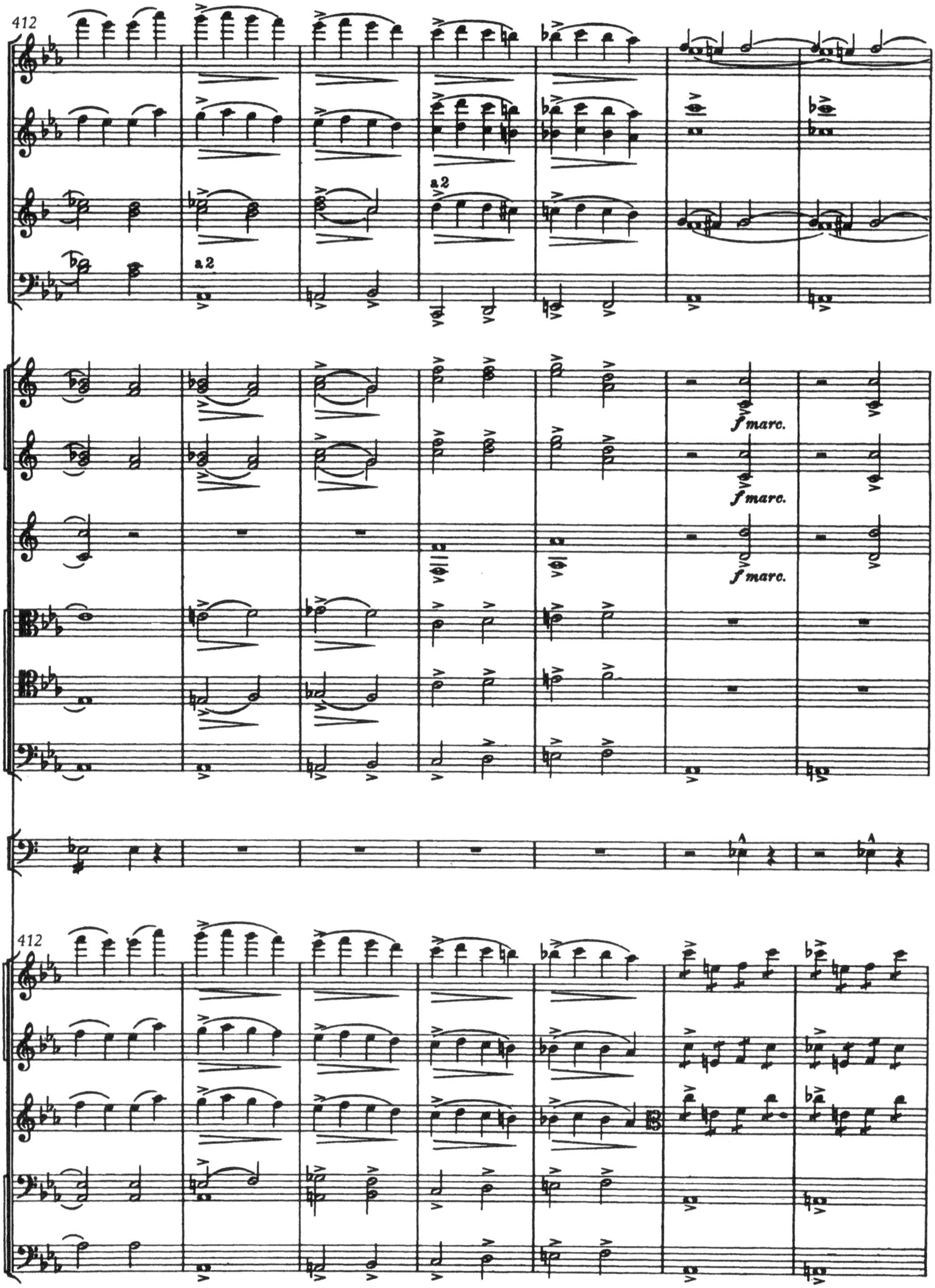
412
a 2
a 2
f marc.
f marc.
f marc.
412

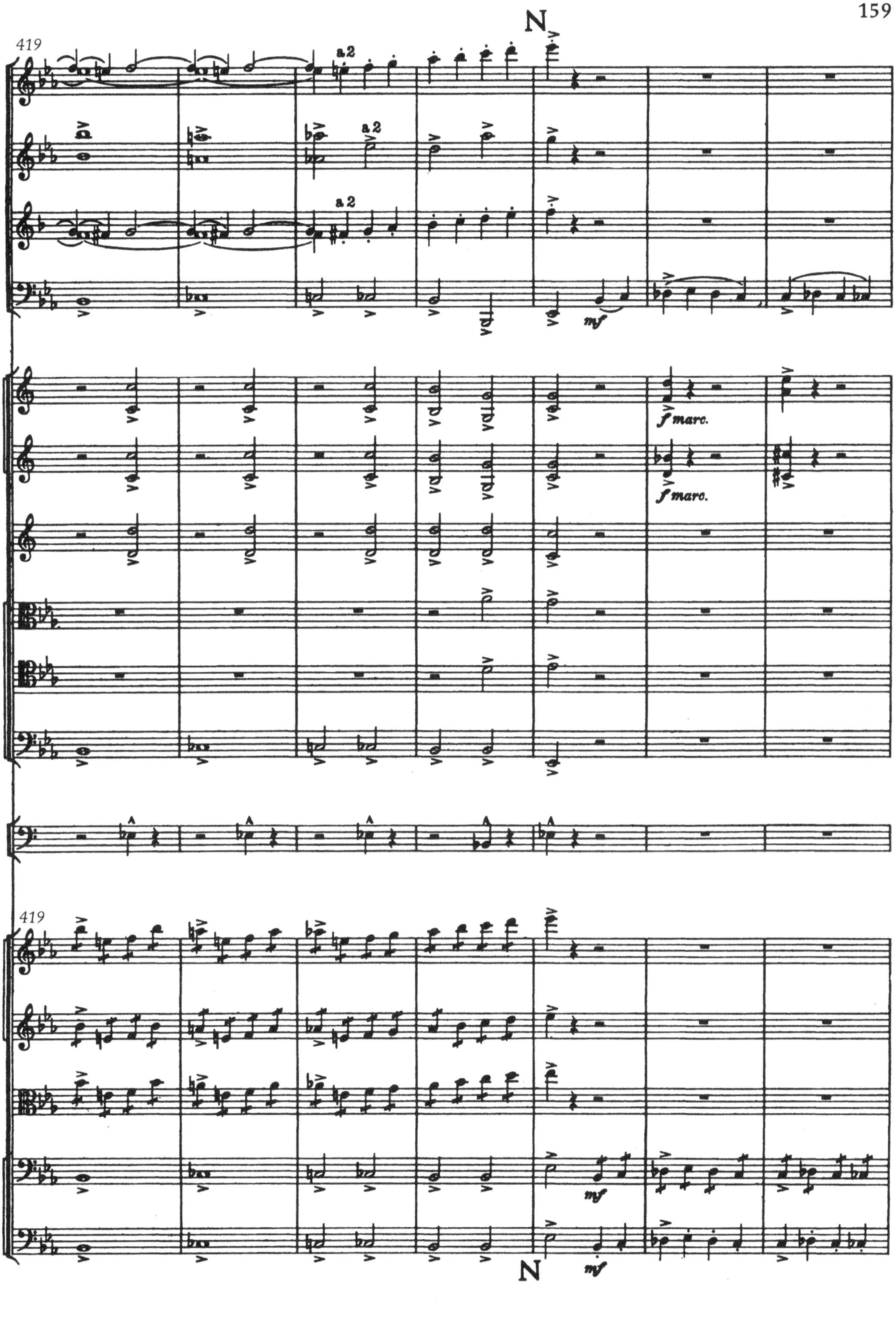
N
419
a 2
a 2
a 2
mf
f marc.
f marc.
419
mf
mf
N

sempre più animato ed accel.

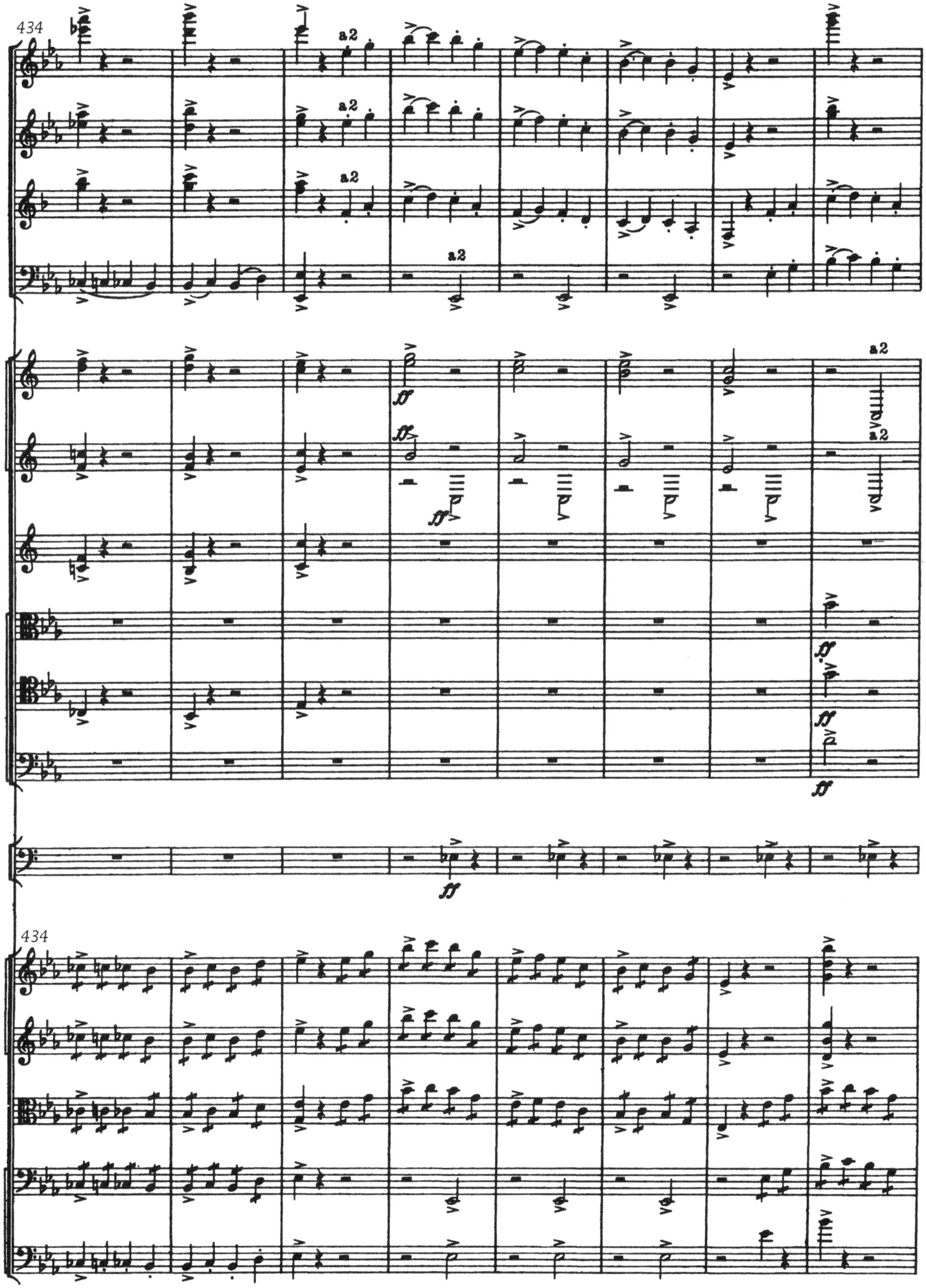
434
a2
a2
a2
a2
ff
ff
ff
a2
a2
ff
ff
ff
ff
434

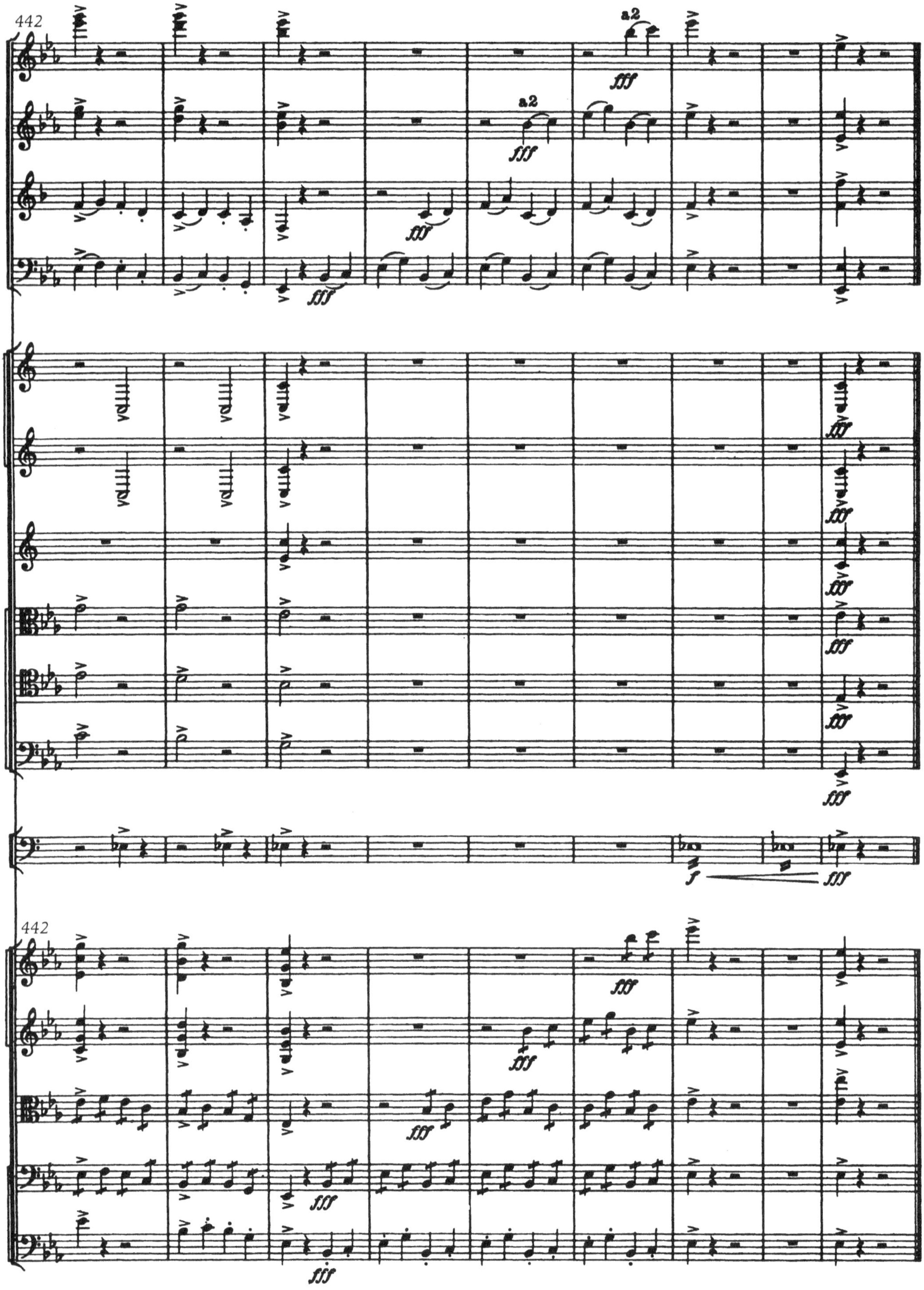
442
a2
a2
fff
f
442

www.ingramcontent.com/pod-product-compliance
Lightning Source LLC
Chambersburg PA
CBHW081136090426
42742CB00015BA/2859